Cyber Threat

DISCARDED

INTERNET SECURITY
FOR HOME
AND BUSINESS

NOV 4 2024

DAVID MCMAHON

Cyber Threat

INTERNET SECURITY
FOR HOME
AND BUSINESS

D A V I D   M C M A H O N

Warwick Publishing Inc.
Toronto Chicago
www.warwickgp.com

Acknowledgments:
Electronic Warfare Associates Canada Ltd.
Canadian Computer Emergency Response Team

Cyber Threat

ISBN: 1-894020-83-9

We acknowledge the financial support of the Government of Canada through the Book Publishing Industry Development Program for our publishing activities.

Published by Warwick Publishing Inc.
162 John Street
Toronto, Ontario M5V 2E5 Canada
www.warwickgp.com

Distributed in the U.S.A. by:
LPC Group
1436 West Randolph Street
Chicago, Illinois 60607

Distributed in Canada by:
General Distribution Services
325 Humber College Blvd.
Toronto, ON M9W 7C3

Cover Design: Kimberley Young
Book Design: Clint Rogerson

Printed and bound in Canada

To my father, for sharing his wisdom

Table of Contents

Foreword 13

Introduction 15

Chapter 1 — The Electronic Landscape:
           A Shared Risk Environment.21

Risk Assessment 23

What Are the Threats? 26

Chapter 2 — Bringing Street Smarts to
           the Information Highway...31

Not Everything is What it Seems 32

Scams 34

E-mail Chain Letters 36

Web Shopping 37

Online Auctions 39

Be Anything You Want to Be 40

Who Are You on the Web? 43

Identity Fraud 46

Your Very Own Web Site 47

Threats from Your Side of the Net 49

Chapter 3 — New Threats from the
           Wired World..............53

Privacy Issues 54

An Unwelcome Visitor: Mobile and Active Code . .56

Trading on the Net 58

Why Me? 60

How Did They Find You? 61

Falling into Software Holes 63

Chapter 4 – Agents of Chaos 65

Threat Agents 66

Who Are Hackers? 66

Hacktivism 70

Web Ethics 72

Script Kiddies 74

Getting Started .76

What Do Hackers Do? 77

Truth and Consequences:
The Case of the Phonemasters 78

Cyber-Criminals .81

Cybotage 82

Cyber-Terrorism .83

Spy vs. Spy 85

Information Warfare 86

The Enemy Within 90

Chapter 5 – Playing Out of Bounds 93

Hacking Wetware: Social Engineering Ploys 93

Dumpster Diving .95

Onsite Tactics 97

Steal the Computer 99

Physical Attack .99

Chapter 6 – The Sorcerer's Apprentice:
            Exploits and Trade Craft .101

The Sorcerer's Apprentice 102

Potions: Malicious Code 102
    Viruses *103*
    Trojan Horses *104*
    Droppers, Logic Bombs, and Worms *104*

Concoctions 105

The Case of Melissa 106

I LOVE YOU. vbs 107

The Virus Business 109

Third-Party Liability 110

Devices 111
    War Dialers *111*
    Vulnerability Scanners *112*
    Computer Microphones *112*

Spells and Incantations 113
    IP Fragmentation *113*
    Ping of Death *114*
    SYNflood *114*
    Storm *115*
    Connection *115*
    Kill Session *116*
    DNS Spoofing *116*

Strategies and Tactics 116
    Reconnaissance *117*

Interception *117*
Insertion and Replay *118*
Delay *119*
Degradation *119*

The Attack 119

Attack Impact 123

Cyber-Espionage 124

Chapter 7 — Surfing with Sharks: A Case Study 127

Chapter 8 — Effective Risk Management . .153

Poachers and Gatekeepers 157

What is Your Risk? .157

Chapter 9 — Practicing Safe Surfing . .159

Information Security 101 159

Procedures and Practices 160

What's the Password? 161
Password Tips *164*

How's Your Browser? 165

Travel Advice for the Information Highway 167
Web Surfing Safety Tips *168*

E-mailing with Confidence 169
E-mail Tips *171*

Contingency Plans and Reaction 172

Backing Up 173

Incident Handling 175

Basic Information 176

What to Do in the Meantime 177

Handling the Intrusion 178

Chapter 10 – Configuring for Self Defense 181

Virus Scanners and E-mmunity 182

Content with Content 183

Firewalls 183

The Next Steps: Detection and Response 187

Intrusion Detection Systems (IDS) 188

Operational Assurance 189

Choosing the Right Person for the Job 190

Making Secure E-Commerce a Reality 191

Secure Transactions .194

Cryptography 195

Public Key Cryptography 197

Digital Signatures 198

Pretty Good Privacy (PGP) 200

Secure Sockets Layer (SSL) 201
Web Certificates *203*
The SSL Process Continues *203*

Brute-Force Code Breaking 204

Beyond SSL 205

Real-Time Credit Card Authorization 205

Public Key Infrastructures (PKIs) 206

RSA-512 Cracked 208

Conclusion 209

Glossary 213

Selected Bibliography 219

Resources 225

Index 233

Foreword

*H*e had written his job title as "Cyberneticist" and I remember looking at his business card for the longest time, thinking. Few people nowadays see their work in these terms. However, David McMahon is not like most people. He works in cyberspace. It is the place where the workforce will be spending more of its time and resources in the future.

As we enter the knowledge age, computers and networks are becoming more and more ubiquitous — even invisible. There should be little doubt in anyone's mind that the influence of computing and the Internet will continue to grow in the course of human work and play. The influence of this technology will evolve to the point where our daily affairs will be acutely dependent on the information infrastructure to support critical decisions. Already, most, if not all of our important "life events" are in some way computer-mediated. Today, many key decisions require the support of a range of information that has been collected, communicated, stored, aggregated, and presented in near real-time across networks of networks.

In *Cyber Threat*, David shares with us more than just another static description of the Internet; he is demonstrating in no uncertain terms how the trust that individuals, organizations, and governments have placed in this new social, political, cultural, and economic space can be subverted by information technology–savvy threats.

For every digital event in cyberspace there is a watcher. It could be a computer process dutifully relaying your e-mail or your Web site requests, but it could also be a sniffer capturing your unencrypted password. In this new conflict space, the goal is control. Where is it? Who has it? How to get it? This is a space in which a crippling denial-of-service attack, from anywhere around the world, is a click away. Consider that in cyberspace it is difficult, if not impossible, to determine the boundaries between organizations — what is "inside" or "outside." In fact, cyberspace is a collective space where we all share each other's risks.

The trends indicate that there is an increasing number of disruptive events generated by individuals who are systematically trying to identify the technical weaknesses in computer systems, or even the more subtle opportunities to socially engineer users into acting on their behalf. Already, the present ranges of action that can be perpetuated extend from hijacking transmissions and defacing Web sites to stealing identities.

In this book, David McMahon not only shows the reader the faces of the threats and their potential impact, but more importantly how to identify them and how to counter them. He transforms the information security agenda from one of "risk avoidance" to that of "risk management." In doing so, he moves everyone up the maturity curve from a state of being a passive participant or unwilling accomplice to that of a knowledgeable and self-reliant netizen.

Robert Garigue
Vice President Information Security, Bank of Montreal
Past Chairman of the Canadian Public Sector CIO Council
Sub-Committee on Information Protection.

Introduction

The use of personal computers and the Internet has grown rapidly in the last decade. Information technology security engineering has become a complex and dynamic field, and threat analysis is now a full-time job. Twenty new malicious software exploits and viruses are released on the Internet every month. Lists of hacked Web pages are compiled by the minute, while computer security advisories are published daily. Academic papers describe new exploits and protective actions in a game of move and countermove — a costly and potentially dangerous game. Threats to Internet security are growing in number, insidiousness, sophistication, and maliciousness of intent. Internet security does not stand still. Indeed, any book on cyber security runs the risk of being obsolete before being printed.

A great many books on Internet security have already been published. Some wrestle with esoteric subjects like quantum cryptography and the heuristics of intrusion detection systems, while others merely touch the surface of the subject. *Cyber Threat* is directed at the middle ground, and is intended for the average Netizen or businessperson who does not have a computer engineering degree or security experience.

Why does the average Net user need a book on cyber security? There are two mistakes computer users make when it comes to Internet security: First, they assume they will not be targeted in cyberspace. But consider that 95 per cent of malicious traffic on the Internet is launched indiscriminately, like random acts of violence on the streets. There is nearly a 100 per cent chance that a home or business user will have their computer scanned for vulnerabilities while connected to the Internet on any given day. The second mistake computer users make is underestimating what they have to lose through a malicious attack on their system or even an unintentional mishap such as a power outage.

One of the main attractions of the Web is its ease of use. Very little computer knowledge is needed now to roam cyberspace or send e-mail. People can use the Net without understanding how it works. But this strength is also its weakness. People focus so much on the positive things that can be done on the Internet that they tend to forget or ignore or fail to learn about the negative things that can happen. The apparent technological sophistication of the Internet may lead the unwary to believe that someone somewhere is running the show. But despite continual efforts by various governments and organizations to regulate activity on the Net, you are on your own in cyberspace. You have very little practical recourse if something goes wrong.

Businesses large and small have been pressured to get on the Net in order to stay competitive. In many cases the bulk of available resources has been directed towards computerization, getting "wired," and trying to keep pace with rapid technological change. There is often little time, money, or thought given to security issues. In small businesses there is rarely a system administrator or technician to turn to if there are problems. Staff are typically given e-mail and Web access in addition to existing computer applications with little or no instruction about safe use. Rarely are there any formal computer security policies or procedures in place. Even in many large computer-dependent organizations, you would be hard pressed to find a systems or network security position. Most people are responsible for their own online security. However, few realize it until something bad happens.

As the Internet becomes more and more integrated with our daily life and commercial activity, the number of things that could go wrong will increase, as will the extent of the damage and the financial impact when they do. In the past two years we have seen the havoc a fairly simple virus can wreak. And while the Y2K issue appears to have been much ado about nothing, the publicity about it made us more aware of how reliant we have become on the Internet. In addition, the growing use of cable modems and DSL lines have made home computers more attractive targets for those wishing to cause chaos. The increased power of home computers that makes access to the Internet faster and easier also increases the speed and ease with which someone with malicious intent can get access to them.

What I have set out to do is to give the reader an appreciation of the magnitude of the cyber threat and to provide some insight into the range of appropriate responses. Risk management is the major theme of this work. Any threat must be considered in the context of the likelihood and potential consequences of its occurrence. It makes no sense to engage in costly threat countermeasures if we are not likely to be targeted or if the consequences of an attack on our system would be tolerable. Internet users must assess their vulnerabilities and the cost and operational impact of an attack on their system before taking protective measures. Many if not most users can provide themselves with adequate protection with comparatively inexpensive software and prescriptive operating practices — that is, practicing safe surfing.

The purpose here is to highlight threats to information security from cyberspace. While there are genuine threats from accidental forces — natural disasters and human errors — I focus on the threats arising from the deliberate misuse of the Internet. This book is not a balanced discussion of the pros and cons of the Internet, e-business, or computing in general. It tells one side of the story — the dark side. The underlying premise is that the role of the Internet in our lives and business is increasingly pervasive and is growing by geometric proportions. The Internet has far more benefits than drawbacks, but if you are going to be out there, you better know the dangers and what you can do about them.

The information I provide in this book is intended as a starting point. It should be sufficient on its own for the average individual user to devise and implement an Internet security plan at home and in their workplace. The self-employed may also find enough here, depending on to what extent they rely on the Internet and e-mail in their business. For the small business owner, or the lucky person who has just been chosen as the office "go-to' person on computer issues, this book will give the background knowledge needed to implement basic security policies. However, it is strongly recommended that if you have networked computers or are planning to sell goods and services over the Net you consult a qualified information security engineer.

Cyber Threat has been reduced from dry texts and overwhelming reams of incomprehensible information into a digestible form. I have used anecdotes and a hypothetical case study to help with the understanding of this complex world. It is my hope that readers will be better able to make a rational decision about their security in cyberspace, and this book will inspire them to take an active interest in their cyber security. I believe it is better that computer users go online with their eyes wide open, albeit with a degree of cynicism, than embrace the technology naïvely.

It is now unsafe to turn on your computer . . .

Chapter 1
The Electronic Landscape:
A "Shared Risk" Environment

The phenomenal growth of the Internet and the outrageous profits being made by dot-com enterprises has created a gold rush mentality in the general populace over the last few years. Everyone wants to get in on the action. Businesses and individuals are racing to stake their claims in cyberspace, plunging into e-commerce with abandon.

Even those who aren't looking to make big money on the Web have nevertheless become intrigued by the possibilities of this new communication realm: The anonymity of the Net can allow the wallflower in real life to become a siren in a chat room; people scattered geographically can create their own virtual communities online, combining their resources and exchanging ideas; dedicated shoppers can browse and make purchases all over the world without ever leaving their comfy chairs; and the number of e-mail messages sent each day now far outstrips the old-fashioned pieces of paper handled by the post office.

The power of the Internet is undeniable. But the fervor with which we've embraced it has blinded many of us to the negative side of all the new opportunities the Internet presents. Like the wild, wild west of old, there are no fixed borders in cyberspace. Open and interconnected systems are coalescing into a rapidly expanding global information infrastructure. Everything is connected, from your telephone to the Tokyo Stock Exchange to the World Wide Web page of a transnational terrorist group. We need to remember that there are both good guys and bad guys in this unregulated and scarcely policed environment. Terms like stealth, firepower, asymmetric threats, and coordinated attacks sound a lot like the air campaign in Yugoslavia, but these are also labels for nefarious Internet activities that can spill over into your computer at home or at work.

The Internet was established by the United States Defense Department in the 1960s. It was to be a communications system that would continue to operate even if one part of it was knocked out. This strength, however, may also be perceived as a weakness. As the Internet has evolved and spread in a gloriously uncontrolled way, the ability for anyone, or any one government, to mediate the activities carried out online has become more and more limited. As citizens have raised concerns about activities on the Net, such as the publishing of pornography, distribution of hate literature, and commission of fraud, governments have passed legislation that attempts to regulate online behavior, but with minimal success so far.

One example is the online casinos based in the Caribbean. Just as these island nations have long offered wealthy North Americans a way of circumventing their nations' tax laws, casinos and other businesses that would be illegal or strictly regulated if physically based in the U.S. or Canada can now serve their North American customers through the Internet from a base offshore without fear of reprisal.

This may seem wonderful for those who believe in a free market, but it may not be so wonderful if you bet a lot of money on one of these foreign-based sites and never receive your winnings. It would be costly and time-consuming to sue a business in a foreign country, and your own country may not be able or willing to offer any help. As this example illustrates, when you are on the Net, you must realize you are entering a "shared risk" environment. Businesses and individuals alike wanting a share of Internet opportunities must also take on the risks involved.

When cautious people hear the word "risk," they tend to want to run the other way. But there is risk inherent in just about every activity we undertake. Most of the time, the positive aspects of an activity outweigh the negative, so we do what we can to reduce the risk, while continuing to enjoy the benefits. For Internet use, this means developing a carefully thought-out security action plan and putting it to work. The first step in such a plan is figuring out what the risks are in your particular situation.

Risk Assessment

Humans are notoriously poor at recognizing real risk and placing it in perspective. We often rely instead on anecdotal evidence to form an opinion and give undue weight to possible consequences, while ignoring the true likelihood of becoming victims of accidental or intentional injury. A typical example is sky diving: most people's instincts would suggest that sky diving is inherently more risky than driving to work every day. But the truth is that, statistically, you are far more likely to die behind the steering wheel of a car, and the impact is the same. Finding the right balance between the likelihood and consequence of an occurrence and putting it in perspective is not always easy, because the result may go against what our intuition or senses tell us.

This is why formal methods were developed for conducting a risk assessment. Briefly, the process consists of a rigorous examination of your assets (the things on which you place value), an identification of who or what might adversely affect your assets (the threats), and a determination of areas in your physical environment and procedures that make you vulnerable to these threats (the vulnerabilities). The threats and vulnerabilities align to form what security specialists call an "exposure." The likelihood that an exposure will be exploited and the potential negative impact if it is form the "intrinsic risk" to your security. After analyzing the value of your assets and the cost of their damage or loss, and comparing it to the cost of applying safeguards, you develop a cost-effective action plan describing what reasonable security measures to take.

So how do we calculate the risks of our using the Internet? There are various risk assessment methods, but they generally break down into either quantitative or qualitative approaches, or a combination of the two. The quantitative approach is used where financial costs can be more easily determined. For example, if your hard drive is wiped out by a particularly nasty virus, how much will it cost to have the data recovered? The qualitative approach deals with less tangible or measurable costs — how worried are you by the prospect of your child being exposed to pornographic images on the Web? What is the cost of lost customer confidence if someone steals credit card numbers from your database?

The extent of the risk assessment will depend on your resources and on how much you rely on the Internet for your activities. Accounting for every possibility and calculating corresponding risk values is an activity best reserved for those with money and time on their hands. The exercise is analogous to asking the question, "What time is it?" Do you want that to the nearest microsecond or rounded to the minute? I have seen risk assessments for a complex system take as much as six months and cost a half a million dollars. On the other hand, some are completed in a couple of days.

In any case, larger organizations with many employees and a complex computer network should have a formal and rigorous risk assessment conducted by security professionals. Most home and small business Internet users have fewer variables to deal with and thus should be able to do their own assessment once they understand the basic processes described in this book. For these users, the risk assessment process can be streamlined; simply ask yourself:

» What have I got to lose?
» What are the chances of being attacked?
» What would be the consequences of such an attack?
» What preventive measures can I afford to undertake?

As I mentioned in the Introduction, a common mistake Internet users make is to underestimate the value of information and computers in their daily life. They also tend to underestimate the likelihood of becoming targets, or they focus on one type of threat, such as computer viruses, and fail to take other possible threats into account.

It has been true in the past that individual and small business computer systems have not been the targets for those who actively prowl the Internet looking to do mischief or real harm. But with the growing use of high-speed Internet connections such as cable modems and DSL lines, home and small business computers have become more enticing. If you use a dial-up modem on a regular phone line to connect to the Net, you are probably only hooked up intermittently. The high-speed connections often operate independently of other communications lines, so many users now have their Internet connection "always on." This factor alone increases the likelihood of being hit by indiscriminate attacks. Hackers are also attracted to these high-speed lines because they can be used to launch mass attacks on Web sites. These are "denial of service" (DoS) attacks in which a Web site is bombarded by huge numbers of access requests that end up blocking legitimate traffic to the site. This is the type of action that was used by hackers to temporarily shut down well known corporate sites like Yahoo and eBay in early 2000.

Another factor that makes home and small business computers ripe for attack through the Internet is their lack of security. Large businesses generally have in-house technical personnel to implement security measures. Greater skill is required to break into their systems. Individuals and smaller businesses tend to lack the knowledge or the resources to set up strong defenses, and thus become vulnerable to even novice hackers.

All of this means that now even small-time computer operators need to make themselves aware of the risks they are exposing themselves to when they use the Internet. With the wide variance in the way the Internet is used by both home and business users, there can be no "one-size-fits-all" risk assessment procedure. Also, your assets, the threats, potential consequences, and preventive measures are constantly changing and evolving, so the risk assessment must be re-done frequently and your security action plan updated accordingly.

What Are the Threats?

The types of cyber threats to your assets fall into these broad categories:

» fraud
» malicious acts
» natural disasters
» theft
» exposure of private information
» sabotage
» human error
» software flaws
» pranks
» misuse of computer systems
» easy accessibility to obscene and other objectionable materials

If you have not implemented any security precautions, or have implemented them in a haphazard, unco-
ordinated way, your assets are vulnerable to these
threats. In computer security terms, a vulnerability is an
intrinsic property of the information, computer system
or network that can be exploited by the bad guys or
which could be adversely affected by an accident, such
as a power outage. A vulnerability, in and of itself, does
not cause harm, it is merely a condition that may lead to
undesirable consequences when affected by natural or
deliberate forces. You should take the time to carefully
scrutinize the setup of your computer systems and
examine how you generally operate. Where are the
holes? Can you fault your online practices? Do you have
bad Web surfing habits that could get you into trouble?
Determining the likelihood of an attack on your assets
often boils down to an educated guess. The process is similar to how you might assess your risk with respect to the
more conventional crime of break and enter. Initially you
may become aware of a significant threat from a large
criminal element operating in your area. The incidence of
break and enter in your district has risen recently due to
factors like low police presence. You are vulnerable in that

your business or home is in a dark area, you have several unbarred windows, and you have no intrusion alarm system. Obviously, it is very likely you will be hit soon, since most of your neighbors have already had problems of this kind, and you are worse off security-wise than they are. When you are hit you may lose thousands of dollars' worth of inventory or have objects of sentimental value destroyed. At the very least you will be left with that horrible feeling of being victimized.

Clearly, this scenario would impress upon you your need for safeguards to reduce your risk. Which safeguards to implement and where would depend on the components of your home or business. If you have windows at street level, you might want to put bars on them. On the other hand, the likelihood of someone climbing up to break in at your second-story windows is slim, so you may determine it's not worth the cost of putting bars on those. You can take a similar approach to securing your computer system. You may find that simple changes in your online practices will be sufficient to protect you from threats to your privacy, for example. Elaborate and expensive encryption software may be unnecessary in your situation.

As you read through this book you will gain a more specific idea of what you want to protect on your computer and how to do it. For now, here are some general points to consider: When evaluating what you have to lose, keep in mind that if you are hooked up to the Internet any data stored on your computer potentially can be stolen, damaged, lost, viewed by strangers, or used in a way you had not authorized. Information you send through e-mail, post on your Web site, or divulge by filling in Web forms or posting in public forums such as newsgroups and chat rooms can be similarly misused. Your ability to filter information that arrives in your home or business is limited.

Legitimate Internet users are, to varying degrees, at the mercy of those who choose to remain anonymous and misuse the Internet for their own advantage. Even where there is no malicious intent, our growing reliance on the Internet makes us susceptible to technical and human errors that can make life in the virtual world difficult. If users — whether individuals or organizations — are to survive the "wild wild Web," they must be prepared, well armed, and nimble. In the chapters that follow, you may be disheartened by the dark and seedy aspects of the Internet I describe. Just remember that there is a great deal more good than bad on the Net. Keep your situation in mind when wading through the threats and vulnerabilities that occupy the vastness of cyberspace. Take what is useful for assessing your own risks. Mitigate and manage those risks within a context that makes good economic sense, and you will be free to enjoy all the good things the Internet has to offer.

Chapter 2
Bringing Street Smarts to the Information Highway

Whenever Internet security is discussed, it's wily hackers who get most of the attention. But the average Internet user is just as likely to fall prey to the same gaggle of con artists, scammers, overzealous salespeople, predators, and just plain jerks that afflict us in real life. Scumbags who once used the telephone or back alley to perpetrate their nefarious schemes have found a remarkable new tool in the Internet. E-mail, chat rooms, bulletin boards, online auction houses — all present the malevolent and anti-social with a whole range of ways to reach the vulnerable. On the Internet they can work with speeds, levels of anonymity, and a geographical range never before available.

But while information technology has given the bad guys new means for their foul deeds, their main tool remains the carelessness of Internet users. The problem is that on the Web, we are lulled into complacency. We're able to roam the Net in seeming anonymity from the comfort of our homes, so we feel we are safe from harm. We forget that that same anonymity is available to the scammer and the mischief-maker. The relative newness of the Internet has led many a user to drop all of the precautions they would normally take when doing similar transactions in the real world. Would you send money offshore to someone you don't know? Buy a "genuine Rolex" from a guy on a street corner? Provide total strangers with intimate details of your life? Allow your child to wander alone in the seedier areas downtown? Not very likely! Yet otherwise intelligent and cautious people do these kinds of things all the time on the Internet. If a stranger on the street told you a wild rumor, would you bother your friends by insisting they pass it on? Yet again, many Internet users forward "spam" (junk e-mail), virus hoaxes, and chain letters this way, thus helping spread and perpetuate viruses and scams.

In subsequent chapters I will discuss the technological devices and techniques used by hackers and other malevolent forces at work on the Web. But in this chapter I will show that by simply bringing the street smarts you use in the real world along with you when you enter the virtual world (and teaching family members and employees to do the same), you can eliminate many of the risks the Internet poses to you or your business.

Not Everything is What it Seems

The first thing to remember when surfing the Web or reading your e-mail messages is that not everyone you encounter is who they say they are or does what they say they will do. It seems like common sense but it's easy to forget when confronted with an enticing e-mail ad or an impressive-looking Web site. This is why con artists have moved their scams online. They can now compose an e-mail ad and mass mail it to millions over the Web for less than the cost of a postage stamp. And you no longer have

Figure 1: A Typical "Spam" E-mail Ad

```
----Original Message -----
```

From: internet-riches5'informatik.uni-olden-burg.de [mailto:internet-riches5'informatik.uni-oldenburg.de]
Sent: Wednesday, January 05, 1994 2:38 PM
To: internet-riches5'informatik.uni-oldenburg.de
Subject: Buy Now A Profitable Internet Business Has You Curious...

Question: Why do SOME PEOPLE SUCCEED in an Internet Business while others fail? The answer is that they have discovered the incredible income potential of DIRECT EMAIL marketing!!!

FREE BUSINESS RESOURCE PACKAGE

***** NOW ONLY $99.00 ****

WARNING! You can purchase this offer whenever you're ready. However, quality e-mail addresses need to be re-harvested every 30 days or less to maintain a good deliverability ratio. This exclusive list is hot NOW!!!

We solicit new members once per year, we can effectively manage only 200 accounts at one time. If you have a product you want to offer to millions of people, OR you are curious as to how people are earning $2,500+ weekly from their home PC, do not wait to get started. TO ORDER these addresses and get the complete business resource package as outlined above, ABSOLUTELY FREE, simply print out the ORDER FORM below and fax it to one of our orders centers. We accept Visa, MasterCard, American Express, Discover & Checks by Fax. Put your initials next to the statement below. ORDER NOW!

to be a computer programmer or graphic designer to create a nice, credible-looking Web site.

Fraud is rampant on the Net, just as it is in the real world. The National Consumers League in the U.S. reported that consumers lost over $3.2 million to Internet fraud in 1999, with an average individual loss of $580. As in the real world, however, though such activities may be illegal, the resources to find and prosecute those responsible are limited. So it is often left to individuals to deal with fraudsters on their own. However, fraudsters use the same psychological techniques online that they use in the real world, and once you understand them and are alert to them, you won't fall for them.

Scams

If you've been on the Web you've no doubt encountered advertisements for online fraud schemes. You may have received them as an e-mail message or seen them posted on electronic bulletin boards or found a Web address for them when you searched a seemingly unrelated topic through a search engine. The people behind them are usually attempting to recruit you for questionable investment schemes and businesses, or to direct you to pornographic Web sites, or to offer you products of dubious quality. Figure 1 is a typical example of an e-mail version.

This message contains many of the elements common to scams, whether online or in the real world, so let's take a moment to analyze it a bit. First of all, it comes from someone I don't know. This should be the first warning sign. The address appears to be in Germany (the ".de" suffix is Germany's national Internet designation). Do I really want to do business with someone I don't know apparently residing in a foreign country? Probably not a good idea. Often when people receive an e-mail from a stranger they assume that it was sent to them personally. If you do not know whom a message is from, regardless of how personable or intriguing it sounds, your correspondent is likely after your money.

Next, look at the subject line. Words and phrases like "Buy Now" and "Profitable" and "Internet Business" create a sense of urgency, appeal to our greed, and pique our curiosity. These are powerful emotions and can often short-circuit our more reasonable faculties. Fraudsters thrive because they know how difficult it is for even intelligent people to resist the lure of easy money or easy weight loss or foolproof ways to get rid of wrinkles or prevent hair loss. Common pitches to business Internet users promote toner cartridges and other business supplies or services such as Web site design at amazingly low costs. We know we should read no further, we know it sounds too good to be true, but still we worry that we might be missing out on something; it probably is a scam, we think, but what if it isn't?

So we take the bait and read on. Hey! It says here we can get something FREE for only $99! What a deal! Use of all-capital letters is another sign to watch for. And once again, we see the urgency appeal — this is a limited-time offer, "do not wait to get started," "order now." High-pressure sales tactics like these are another danger sign. Then there's the promise of easy money — "people are earning $2,500 + weekly working from their home PCs." Finally, all we have to do is fax information about ourselves as well as our credit card or bank account information — the request for money.

Now let's think about what's not in this message: no phone number to call for more information, and no physical address for the company. A legitimate business would provide these. Always beware of messages like this one. Many are just ploys to get your credit card number, which can then be used fraudulently. In the case of Figure 1, the sender seems to be trying to recruit members to recruit even more members in an illegal pyramid scheme.

E-mail Chain Letters

Another popular online swindle technique is to appeal to your better emotions, like asking for charitable donations or selling items that purportedly benefit non-profit groups. Sometimes these requests come in the form of e-mail chain letters that ask you to forward them to your friends. For the superstitious, chain letters also contain some dire warning of what will happen if you fail to pass it along and the chain gets broken. As well as playing on your sympathy to squeeze money out of you, such techniques are also used to spread rumors about certain corporations or organizations or their products, or to harass someone by getting masses of people to complain to their e-mail address. There has also been the "computer virus" hoax variation, which warns you to tell all your friends about a dangerous virus that's activated when you open a certain type of e-mail. Treat e-mails like these as you would junk mail — send them directly to your recycle bin. Do not forward them to your friends.

And incidentally, if you think this would be a good technique for promoting genuine, constructive causes, think again. A teacher in Nova Scotia decided to use e-mail as a research project for her geography class. She had each student send an e-mail to someone they knew, asking them to respond with information about their region or country, and in turn to forward the message to people they knew. Within days the class's e-mail address was swamped with responses from all over the world, and the teacher had to close the e-mail address altogether.

Web Shopping

The most common Internet consumer fraud is the failure to deliver goods paid for. You may have purchased a product advertised in an e-mail like Figure 1 or through a Web site ad. It may have all seemed very legitimate. But once again, remember that it is very easy to set up a sophisticated-looking Web site. Always check out the seller before you buy anything online. Try to find out who it is you're dealing with by phoning them or requesting additional information by mail. If they are reluctant to give you solid information regarding money-back guarantees and specific delivery dates, don't send them your money.

The primary method of payment for goods bought over the Web is through credit cards. If you do decide to make a purchase from an online seller (after determining they are legitimate), this is probably the best payment method, since it does offer some recourse if things go awry. You have a record of the transaction and you can dispute an inflated charge or charges for goods not received. Also, companies have to fulfill certain criteria of reliability and stability before they are given a credit card account, so there's less chance they will magically "disappear" once they have your money.

Even so, it should come as no surprise that credit card companies report that the vast majority of all billing disputes involve online purchases. I have experienced this first hand, although the disputes I've been involved in were due not to fraud but to glitches in the payment mechanism of a company's Web server, which billed me a dozen times for the same item. Normally, these transactions are straightforward to identify and refute, but nevertheless they are inconvenient for both the consumer and the credit card company.

Even when you receive the item you ordered over the Web, it may not be exactly as advertised. I have been caught out twice buying software — from established companies — that did not match the functionality purported on their Web site. How do you return software that you downloaded over the Web? Make sure the company you deal with has a convenient returns policy.

It helps if you can check out a product in the real world before purchasing it online, but increasingly you have no choice. I recently purchased a $50 piece of software from a Fortune 500 Canadian company located just 10 km from where I live. This company operates no retail stores and it was only possible to order new products online, so that's what I did. I agreed to pay $50 for the software upgrade and have it delivered by post to my doorstep. What happened next was typical of many online retail transactions. This company had subcontracted its e-business operations to a firm in the U.S.A. which processed my order, shipped it from a warehouse thousands of miles away using a standing arrangement with a courier of choice, who in turn employed a customs broker . . . and so on and so forth. Along the way, the original $50 Canadian price magically turned into $50 US; add courier costs, customs duties (so much for free trade), taxes on the taxes, and I ended up with a bill for $125. In some cases, e-commerce is keeping many people employed! When you make an online purchase, be sure all charges have been included in the final quoted price.

Are you sure what you've purchased is legal? The Internet has proven a wonderful way of dumping stolen goods. You may rejoice in getting that DVD player for next to nothing, but might want to question why it was so cheap. There's a chance the police may show up one day to confiscate it. The Internet also facilitates the sale of goods that may not be legally sold in your country. Prescription drugs are a prime example. There is no obvious storefront and the transaction often bypasses customs. As well as possibly being illegal, how can you be sure the drug is what the seller says it is? How does the seller ensure the quality and strength of the product? Unless you have your own testing lab, you might want to think twice about purchasing medical supplies this way.

Online Auctions

Sometimes as you shop online, you'll find you are not dealing with a commercial entity but an individual. The Internet made the notion of a global village a reality; it was not long before someone thought of setting up an online yard sale. The buying and selling of collectibles and second-hand goods has become a very popular activity on the Web. Online auction houses such as eBay have picked up on the idea of brokering the exchange of goods made so much more convenient and profitable by the Net. Generally, these auction sites work by allowing someone to post an item for sale and anyone else to place a bid for the item. The auction house manages the auction process; receiving payment and getting the purchased item is left to the buyer and seller involved. Usually everyone is satisfied.

Even so, the National Consumer League cited online auctions as the fastest-growing type of fraud on the Internet. Partly this has to do with the incredible volume of online bids. Ebay has a few million items listed on its site, and 650 bids are placed every minute. Chances are that a few of these are not entirely honest. Some sellers hide their true identity. They may practice "shill" bidding — placing bids on their own item to boost its bidding price. The goods they're offering may be bogus or stolen. Some buyers may try to pay with forged money orders, stolen credit cards or rubber checks. Well-established auction sites like eBay do what they can to limit these practices, and other Net entrepreneurs have geared up to address these problems; one example is the online escrow service, where payment can be held by a third party until the item purchased is received and found to be satisfactory. You may want to take advantage of this service for more expensive items (the fee may not be worth that genuine, original Pet Rock you bid $5 for).

Be Anything You Want to Be

On the Web, individuals can pretend to be whomever or whatever they want. The anonymity of the Internet permits anyone to adopt any persona they wish. Most users adopt an online personality that is not exactly that of their real self. It is part of the fun of the Internet and usually no harm is done by it.

But of course there are some people who will deliberately use the cloak of cyberspace to hide their true intentions. For example, it is a relatively easy matter for a 50-year-old man to masquerade as a 10-year-old girl. Unfortunately, pedophiles have taken to the Internet. Their favorite haunts are the chat rooms, the popular term for Internet Relay Chat (IRC). These are real-time channels on the Internet through which many people can converse at any given time — much like a conference call or party line. At present, the chat is usually not verbal but via the keyboard, which can help to cover a participant's true identity. There are thousands of chat rooms covering every topic imaginable. You get into these chat rooms either through your browser or with special IRC software. It is also possible to establish a private chat with another user.

Chat rooms can be exciting and rough places. Participants can get involved in heated online debates; sometimes things get ugly. Some users enjoy deliberately provoking their fellow participants with outrageous or nasty statements. Some use the chat room to convert and recruit members to fringe organizations such as neo-Nazi groups. And others use chat to establish contact with the vulnerable and lonely, usually with sinister motives in mind. Pedophiles, for example, typically will frequent popular children's channels, often sitting in the background unnoticed ("lurking" in chat room parlance), just listening and sizing up the participants. They then gradually introduce themselves into the conversation and establish themselves as another kid. Eventually, the pedophile will want to either lure a child into a private chat room and talk dirty or entice the victim into meeting in real life — sometimes traveling hundreds of miles to do so. I know of several police forces that have begun to play the deception game too in chat rooms, to identify and arrest potential pedophiles.

Obviously, you will want to protect young children from these predators. But the challenge becomes clear when so many adults fall for similar ploys. Hollywood movies like *You Have Mail* play up the idea of the Internet as an ideal matchmaker. As with the risk posed by pedophiles, the single Internet user needs to be aware of lonely heart scams. The threat motivation can vary. Individuals can be befriended and enticed into departing with their money, or they may be lured into meeting in real life, with deadly consequences.

Social interaction — the good as well as the bad — is one of the most popular activities on the Net. We also value the Internet for the access it gives us to an incredible wealth of information. Sifting through the material and determining what is useful and what is not can be a major task. We have all heard the story about people buying their degrees from some pseudo-university and practicing their profession for years before being caught. The one thing you will notice on the Web is that everyone seems to be an expert, or at least have something to say. Visit any newsgroup relating to a subject that you already know quite well. You will notice that there are many people talking about subject matter that clearly they know very little about. Occasionally, the real experts emerge to say their piece and then retire from the discussion thread.

You can go to any number of sites on the Internet and find people claiming to be lawyers dispensing free legal advice over the Web. It is said that "free advice is worth what you paid for it." Even if the person at the other keyboard is a real lawyer (which is difficult to prove), their legal advice is likely specific to their country or state law. Canadian divorce or copyright laws probably have no applicability in Norway, for instance.

Finance and health are other areas in which you have to be particularly careful in evaluating online information. If it is not a get-rich-quick scheme then it is a lose-weight-fast diet plan. The qualifications and real-world track records of the the individuals offering you their advice need to be established. Do not assume that grand claims must be legitimate merely because they are presented on a professional-looking Web site. Where a particular product is advocated in a seemingly non-commercial Web site, look more carefully at site sponsors and copyright notices. Chances are that the site is in fact funded by the maker of the product, so the information provided must be treated with healthy skepticism.

Chat rooms are also frequently used by those with less dire but still annoying ulterior motives like promoting a stock or putting a public relations spin on products, companies, and politicians. Sometimes these attempts are clumsy and obvious, but others can be quite slick and effective. Unlike other media that have editors or moderators ensuring a measure of objectivity, chat rooms and message boards often have little supervision. When there is someone overseeing things, their intervention is usually limited to maintaining set codes of conduct in language use and etiquette. Judging the validity of the content is left to the participants themselves.

Cyberspace is full of bogus claims, misinformation, and uninformed discourse. A small portion can be attributable to deliberate deception. The best practice is to verify the reputation of the source of the information and cross-reference with independent sources, though, as I will discuss later, even reputable information sources can be duped or have their Web sites altered to display inaccurate information. The novelty and anonymity of Internet communications make it easy to abuse or mar a corporation's image or criticize a public figure. You should take this into account when reading others' remarks or when contemplating making your own opinion heard. Remember that libel laws can apply on the Net as elsewhere, and big corporations and wealthy individuals have the means to track you down if you make false statements about them or their products. Suits against disgruntled employees who have started rumors in chat rooms and dissatisfied customers who have put up Web sites that tarnish a company's image have been successfully pursued through the courts.

Who Are You on the Web?

As I mentioned above, people's online personalities are often different from their real world versions. This sometimes may be part of ploy to commit fraud or perpetrate other unethical or illegal activities. Usually, though, it is just a way for people to free themselves from societal stereotypes or assumptions they feel are made about them when they interact face to face. It can be an interesting experiment to see how you are treated when you present yourself as someone of a different race or the opposite sex. Sometimes the change is not so deliberate; people simply become less cautious or restrained on the Web than they are in real life. Again, they get lulled by that feeling of security and anonymity.

Falling unwittingly into this trap can have unintended, sometimes severe consequences for your real-world self. It is wise to take a moment before posting a message on the Web that expresses a strong opinion or contains language or subject matter that others may find offensive. Would you make these comments if you were conversing with strangers in a cafe? Would you care if others overheard? Would it bother you if your kids, spouse, neighbors, boss, clients, or other people whose opinion you value read your comments? If so, don't press that send button!

Remember that the Internet has a long memory. All information written in cyberspace is ultimately readable from a Web browser. Internet applications such as gopher, Archie, news, e-mail, IRC, and many more have essentially merged into Web browsers. Just because it was typed in an IRC session, or sent via an e-mail or attachment does not mean that it will not show up at some time in the future when someone types key words into a popular search engine. Information and confidences have a way of being easily shared over the Net. A good rule of thumb is never write anything down on the Internet which you could not handle becoming public.

Many people are far too cavalier in the manner in which they exchange words on the Internet. The communication is no less real over the Internet than it would be face to face in real life. However, sitting behind a terminal in the remoteness of an office cubicle or at home often distances us from the reality of the exchange. Expressing an objectionable opinion about a person or product and posting it to a newsgroup, chat discussion, Web site or other public forum is analogous to taking out an ad in an internationally read newspaper and can open you up to charges of libel. Even private e-mail can find its way accidentally to distribution lists and out into the public.

For those with the courage of their convictions and force of opinion, posting to a public site like a newsgroup will likely draw lively discussion. If your opinion is radically different from the norm you might expect numerous e-mails or postings expressing outrage that can get fairly personal. "Flame wars" are not uncommon in highly opinionated groups. What goes around comes around a thousand-fold. You might also become the target of an e-mail "bomb"; not at all as dangerous as the real thing, but a major annoyance — someone you antagonized may assault your e-mail address with a ton of e-mail messages, causing it to be overloaded and blocking out legitimate communications. Receiving hate e-mail and being "stalked" via the Web are also possible unpleasant consequences of posting thoughtless remarks.

Aside from censoring your posts, you can avoid or limit counter-attacks by using different e-mail addresses for different purposes. Keep your private addresses for your friends and meaningful correspondence. Get a free e-mail address from services like Hotmail.com for BBS postings and other types of public exchanges. If you catch some heat or attract other unwanted attention, you can easily cancel the free address, without messing up your more important e-mail connection. Also, junk e-mailers often get their target addresses from newsgroup and chat room postings — another good reason to have multiple e-mail addresses that you can close or ignore without hampering your more important communications.

Identity Fraud

By now you know that people often pretend to be something they're not on the Internet. In addition to pretending to be someone else, however, they may pretend to be *you*, using information stolen from databases and gathered from comments you've made in seemingly innocuous forums. Identity fraud has been around a long time, but as with other types of fraud it is made much easier by the Internet, where otherwise private information is not treated with the care it should be.

Avoid giving personal information out on the Internet. Remember, you are talking to strangers and you do not know where this information will end up. Personal identification information, such as addresses, phone numbers, birth dates, and social insurance/security numbers, is often collected or sold over the Web. With this information strangers can take advantage of your clean driving record, your good credit rating, your professional reputation, to perpetrate fraud in your name.

Theft of identity is one of the greatest dangers to private individuals from the Web, and one of the most frustrating to rectify. The repercussions can haunt you for years. Getting loans, renting cars and apartments, getting credit cards — all can be made difficult or impossible if someone destroys your credit rating by using your name for fraudulent purposes. In one extreme example, a victim of identity theft was arrested two or three times because his "double" was on police wanted lists. Whenever the innocent man's driver's license was checked on police files, he would be hauled in for questioning.

Fraudulent use of your commercial identity may also occur on the Net, damaging your business's reputation and the confidence of your customers. As I've mentioned before, it is very easy to set up a Web site; pranksters and others can set up sites with names that are very similar to that of your business or organization. When someone wants to get to your site but types in the fake name by mistake, they are routed to the fake site. The goal of hijacking your potential clients may be just to perpetrate a prank. It may also be a way to protest something your business does. Even more troubling, it may be a ploy by a competitor to discredit you or your business, or an attempt to defraud your customers by making them think they are dealing with you.

Vigilance is about the only way to deal with these schemes. Some larger corporations employ outside firms to constantly search the Net for instances of unauthorized use of their trademarks. This may be beyond your means, but you can do occasional searches yourself or appoint one of your employees to do so. Also, respond quickly to complaints from customers who encounter these bogus sites.

Your Very Own Web Site

It is not uncommon to have a Web site these days, as an individual or for business purposes. Software has been developed that makes it easy enough for computer-literate ten-year-olds to create their own sites in a day. With this simplicity, however, comes the temptation to put up a site before giving careful thought to its contents. Again, you may end up giving an impression you hadn't intended. Thinking of linking your site to all sorts of external Web sites, for example? Consider where those links may lead. In many people's minds a link represents endorsement of the external site, its material and all of its links. If you do include links on your site check them every so often to see where they lead (remember that the content of your linked sites is always subject to change). Furthermore, for neophyte Web users it is not always obvious where your Web site ends and someone else's begins. Many times, I have received e-mails from visitors with questions unrelated to the sites that I manage, simply because they got disorientated in their surfing.

As with postings to chat rooms and other public forums, the content of your Web site is being archived somewhere and may be accessible even after you remove it — another reason to exercise caution when deciding on the content of your site.

An additional concern is the inclusion of copyrighted material on your site. It is very easy to copy images and text from one site and use it on another. With all this cutting and pasting that makes its way into school homework assignments or corporate reports, it is increasingly difficult to tell who copied whom. I have seen it come full circle, where something I once wrote ended up in a competitor's report to a mutual client. Often in my work it is difficult to track down the original source of the information to verify authenticity or request permission to reuse it. If you use someone else's work on your Web site, make sure you have their permission to do so, or can show that you made an effort to contact the copyright owner. If you receive a complaint about unauthorized use of copyrighted material, remove it immediately.

Conversely, be aware that material you post on your site may be "borrowed" in turn by someone else for use on theirs. If you have a professional photography business, for instance, a Web site is a great way to display examples of your work. But you also stand a good chance of having any images you display reproduced elsewhere without your consent or any compensation. Usually it is enough to contact the Web site's creator and inform them that they have violated your copyright. Threatening a lawsuit may help against the more stubborn, but actually suing is usually more costly and time-consuming than it's worth. There are software packages that prevent electronic cut and pasting or copying, though they do not prevent someone from just retyping the whole thing or scanning a printed version and posting that on a Web site.

Putting a copyright notice on original photos, illustrations and text may help by reminding people that it's illegal to use your work without permission. All trademark and copyright laws substantiated in real life apply on the Internet. It is enforcing them that is difficult. Establishing a trade name is only the beginning; having the money to defend it is most of the battle. I had the name of my first home business trademarked, but that did not stop a candy bar company from using the name three years later for one of their products and sending me an e-mail demanding that I take down my Web site of the same name.

If you try and register a domain name for your web site (www.mycompany.com) you will find that nearly all words in the dictionary have been taken already, primarily by people who registered everything they could think of in hopes that someone will want the name badly enough to pay them big bucks for it. The practice is called "cyber-squatting." Some squatters were bold enough to register many Fortune 100 company names, only to be sued for trade name violation. Unlike most individuals and small businesses, big corporations have the means and the will to pursue lengthy court cases, so be careful when using well-known trademarks on your site.

Threats from Your Side of the Net

As well as being the target of malicious or fraudulent behavior, your computer can be a source of it. Children and employees may use your computer and Internet connection in ways you were unaware of. However, you may end up being the one to suffer some of the consequences of their actions. The notion that parents or legal guardians are responsible for their children's actions is widely accepted. The law also extends to the Internet. If your kid just downloaded a hacking program from the Web and launched it at Corporation X, it is your computer that the police are going to confiscate and you who may have to pay for damages.

How much trouble can your young teenager get into alone in his room? Robert Masse was 15 years old when he penetrated a plethora of government and commercial computer systems, including that of the federal auditor general.

"You don't see what you are doing. I caused a lot of problems. I was costing companies money. Racking up large long-distance bills . . . eating up a small company's telecommunications budget. There's no face to associate the problems you're causing," Robert would later say.

It was during the cold war when Masse broke into USSR research computers and alarms went off in the Western and Eastern security and intelligence agencies. His activities were traced to his Montreal home telephone number registered to his father who, to make matters worse, worked for the federal police force and was placed under investigation for espionage. The Royal Canadian Mounted Police (RCMP) security service (the equivalent to the FBI) came knocking one day with a search warrant. Computers, media, peripherals, and accessories were seized from the family.

"My mom and sister were crying. My dad had a look on his face that I had never seen before. It was a look of disappointment. That's what hit me hard. Any excitement I had, or feelings that this was cool, were erased," Masse recounted in an interview with Canadian Press nine years later.

Children generally lack the life experience to foresee the potential consequences of their acts. Adults, however, should be expected to know better. The difference is that adults will likely be more adept at hiding their identity and covering up their tracks. Many cyber threats to a company or organization originate with insiders — disgruntled employees who intentionally bad-mouth your company in chat rooms or leak confidential information, or others who use corporate e-mail and Internet connections to perpetrate fraud, harass fellow workers and view inappropriate Web sites. There have been a few cases where employees of government or corporate entities used their employers' e-mail facilities to distribute child pornography or other objectionable material.

Simple carelessness can be another source of woe. A secret Nova Scotia government document was leaked in December 1999 when an e-mail message that should have gone to Paul *MacEachern,* communications officer, went to Paul *MacEwan,* opposition MLA, instead. Old e-mails have also figured prominently in recent investigations, such as the Microsoft antitrust case and the Monica Lewinsky investigation. You and your employees should remember that e-mail is not the best way to send sensitive information. It should be treated like a postcard — the message is potentially readable by anyone who happens to see it. Also, without specific measures to destroy them, e-mails can persist for a long time in cyberspace and on your computer system, even after you think you have deleted them.

If you are not the only one using your computer and Internet address, or whenever you bear the responsibility for how they are used, it is important to establish clear guidelines for their use. Where possible, do not allow the computer to be used without supervision, especially where children are involved. If you find that a child or someone else is attempting to hide their Internet activities, there's a good chance they're doing something they know you would not approve of. Talk to family members and employees about online dangers so that they won't unknowingly expose themselves or your company to harm. Keep communication pathways open so that they can come to you if they encounter something disturbing or inadvertently get involved in a dangerous situation online.

Chapter 3
New Threats from the Wired World

*I*n chapter 2 we saw how the same old scams, hoaxes, and trickery are perpetrated with the help of the Internet and the artificial sense of security it can give users. In this chapter we will explore the technological capabilities of the Internet that allows those so inclined to wreak havoc, rip you off, and do serious damage to you or your company's credibility and productivity.

Many of these methods and devices still play on people's gullibility and carelessness. But in addition, there is the average Internet user's ignorance of how e-mails, Internet browsers, and networks actually work. After reading chapter 2, you know that things and people you discover on the Web are not always what they seem, that you must think carefully before revealing information about yourself or your company for e-mails or online forums, and that you need to do some additional research before sending off a check or giving out your credit card number to a person or company you found on the Web.

But there are additional precautions to transfer from real life to the Net, once you understand the way e-mail and Web sites work. Would you open a package from someone you never heard of with no return address? If the contents had a button on it that said PRESS ME — would you? Yet many people have no reluctance in opening and executing anonymous programs from e-mail attachments, thus spreading the impact of computer viruses.

Privacy Issues

Different people have different degrees of concern about their privacy. Some don't mind having their phone number in the phone book and are willing to accept the annoyance of telemarketing calls in exchange for providing an easy way for their friends to contact them. Others view phone calls from strangers as an intrusion and therefore decide to have an unlisted number. It's the same on the Internet. Each user has to decide how much information about themselves they want floating about in cyberspace. Whatever your feelings on the issue, it's important to know the methods strangers can use to find out more about you through the Web. Some of these people may simply want to sell stuff to you; others may have more sinister motives.

Privacy is something many of us take for granted. That is, until it has been violated. There is still a reasonable expectation of privacy when sending e-mail. But in reality e-mail is akin to holding a private conversation in a restaurant or talking on a cellular phone. Polite people do not eavesdrop. But current privacy mechanisms in e-mail programs only keep the polite people out. To steal people's e-mail, you still have to do a bit of work, but there are people willing to do that work.

In August 1999, the confidentiality of over fifty million e-mail accounts worldwide was compromised by a group calling itself "Hackers Unite." Seven Americans and a

Swede took advantage of code supposedly left over from development, typed in the secret password "eh" — good for all Hotmail accounts — together with the username, and they were in. "How to"instructions were posted on the Net, and news of the stunt spread like wildfire.

In the previous chapter, I discussed how information abut you can be gleaned form your online postings. This is a fairly simple procedure that only requires an ability to read. But there are more insidious means and devices that allow others to encroach into your life and meddle in your affairs. The software most of us use in the office and home is configured to serve our best interests, but do you trust some large corporation to determine what is best for you? Your visit is logged on the remote Web server when you visit a Web site. Your Internet Protocol (IP) address and the domain is recorded, as is the version of browser, operating system, the length of stay, what pages you viewed and for how long, the previous site you visited and, of course, anything you type into Web forms while you are on that site.

Something called a "cookie" is created with a subset of this information and is transferred and stored on your computer. The ostensible reason Web masters use cookies is to identify your settings and preferences so that you don't have to reset them each time you go to their sites or to preserve the state of your browsing session and choices as you navigate through the site. Cookies could have been a good thing if it were not for the potential for serious exploitation. The danger is that the confidential information that you typed into a page, like the account and password or your credit card number, can be stored in plaintext in a cookie without you knowing. It is possible for others, with a bit of ingenuity, to read these cookies off your system from a remote server during your Web browsing session.

Here is a nightmare example: Suppose you just bought an item online. You presumed that the transaction was secure because the site said so, and you trust the vendor's word. Then you go to another less reputable site by choice, by accident, or by being directed there through domain name service (DNS) "spoofing" (a common re-routing ploy). This seedy site reads your cookie files, and steals your credit card number and your surfing habits. Your card number is worth your credit limit on the black market. This is what Eric Schmidt, the chief executive officer of Novell, claims happened to him when his credit card was stolen online. He called cookies "one of the disasters for computers."

You may be surprised to learn that there's a big business in using cookies to assemble your consumer profile and selling it to direct sales marketers sorted by consumers, zip/postal code, and buying habits. You may regard this as a mere annoyance, but what if the buyer is a potential employer wanting to know what you do on the Web? What if it's an insurance company — your visit to the hepatitis C information Web site may be of great interest to them. There have been legislative attempts to limit the use of this type of information, but once again enforcement of national laws is very difficult in the globalized Internet. Catching law breakers is often left to the vigilance of users and non-profit citizen privacy organizations. The good news is that cookies can be rejected. The bad news is that your browser is set by default to accept cookies and a lot more.

An Unwelcome Visitor: Mobile and Active Code

Many e-mail programs automatically display messages written in hypertext markup language (HTML), the same text-based language used by Web pages. Mobile code (Java, Active X) is special software than can be downloaded by the distant Web server to your computer and executed automatically without you even knowing. They too are set to run by default and can be turned off. It is possible to embed mobile code into an e-mail and have it run. The ramifications are that you could have a software program execute automatically when you open your e-mail. The most common way of infecting computers with malicious code such as viruses is to send them as e-mail attachments and trick users into double-clicking on them to execute the malicious code. In the future, these nasty things may be able to launch themselves when a user merely opens an e-mail message.

A lot of the software we use is not set up to handle these nasties. Do not presuppose that software developers have security in mind when their product is built. Functionality and security are more often found in two distant camps, one in revenue, the other in expense.

You can get a window on what is really happening by installing a program that regulates network access to your computer, such as a firewall. A firewall maintains a log of all incoming attempts to gain access to your computer through your Internet connection. In the process of monitoring traffic on my personal firewall it became evident that many operating systems (and other) programs like to call home. Perhaps it is to check and see whether it is in your best interest to update your browser or e-mail software. Personally, I find this distressing and I block any unsolicited connection attempts by my computer's software to remote places.

How do these hackers and other threat agents hunt your computer down? A machine address (MAC) is an unique serial number burned into your network interface card. It is therefore bound physically to your personal computer and can indirectly identify its user. Microsoft

embeds the MAC in Microsoft Office documents to identify the writer. Beware, a document written on a computer can be traced back to that particular computer, unless
steps are taken to scrub the references. New computer
chips will also have this unique ID, like the registration
number on your car, but harder to file off.

The next version of the Internet addressing protocols
(TCP/IP) will have the capability to insert the MAC as a
portion of the address. This is not necessarily a bad thing.
The instances of crank telephone calls dropped when
caller ID came into use. Similarly, by including the MAC in
e-mails, newsgroup postings, and other Internet traffic it
is hoped spamming (junk e-mail), Internet fraud, and
hacking will be shut down by raising the specter of trace-
ability. The industrious hacker will be able to get around
this mechanism, but it will still catch a lot of bad actors.

You, as a legitimate user, need to be aware of the
decreased level of anonymity. There are still ways of hiding your identity if you need to do so. Freedom of speech
has been one of the tenets of the Internet mindset, supported by the anonymity afforded by cyberspace. For
this reason and others, services have sprung up that
allow Internet users to e-mail or Web surf in anonymity.
These "anonymizers" work by providing an e-mail or
Web-browsing proxy where your real address is stripped
off and a fictitious return address inserted. To ensure the
integrity of the operation, the entire process should be
automated and encrypted so that no human can retrace
the association between your address and the assigned
one. For the paranoid, you can route your message
through a dozen anonymizers in as many countries.

Trading on the Net

The stock market has been greatly affected by the
Internet. Dot-com stocks have driven the markets to new

heights. It seems like if you're not actually starting an Internet business, you're investing in one you hope will become the next Microsoft. As in many other areas, the Internet's ease of use has led some people into deep investment waters before they've learned to swim. Many people collect investment advice from various sources on the Web, some of which are not very reliable. Law enforcement agencies in their annual reports have noted that securities fraud on the Internet is increasing. The value of some stocks has been manipulated by rumors circulated in newsgroups and chat rooms. These rumors can spark frantic trading, especially on Internet stock trading sites that lack educated brokers to moderate the information. There have even been cases of dormant or non-existent stock being traded over the Internet.

For these reasons, concerns have been raised about the practice of day trading, where individuals with limited training make their own buy and sell orders for their stock portfolios. For some it has paid off; others have been destroyed by financial losses and the stress of the frantic-paced trading. The most extreme example, of course, has been Mark Barton, the man who went on a rampage at his day-trading office in August 1999 in Atlanta, killing several people including himself.

On the other hand, some take the high pressure into stride and incorporate it into their trading methods. I mentioned earlier how easy it is to sell contraband on the Net or to sell nothing for something. The Internet has also permitted a new take on an old trick called kiting. The old example would be to write yourself a check for $1000 from one account and deposit it in another, then write another check to cover the first check and so on. In the past the delay in tracing the integrity of the deposits could be long enough such that the first check would clear before the final deposit had been verified. In one Internet version of this scam, stocks are traded at a rate faster than payments can be verified. Dealing with the problem is particularly daunting when you consider the global nature of the Internet; the different time zones make it a challenge to coordinate timing to within a few seconds across large networks.

Why Me?

Why would anyone want to break into your machine at home? After all, you probably don't have valuable industrial secrets or customer databases to spy on. Like computer virus, direct attacks on your system are often just random and not aimed at you personally (if that's any comfort). Some attacks are like the work of graffiti artists in the streets — you had a blank wall, so they used it. As technology becomes more sophisticated and more affordable for individual users, home computer systems will become more attractive. Instead of annoying but usually harmless pranks, home users may be subject to more serious crimes — the cyber equivalent of stealing your car and using it in a robbery or a hit-and-run. Right now, threat agents seem to be increasingly targeting home computers that have high-speed connections like ISDN, DSL or cable modems. One reason is the speed: many more attacks can be launched per second from a fast connection. Many denial of service attacks rely on fast throughput to be effective and flood the victim computer with data. These fast connections are also always on. The window of opportunity is always open and the user is not always home.

Cable modems are extremely fast, so many of us have them, but there are intrinsic properties of these devices that make them vulnerable. Along with the potential hijacking of your system, there are increased threats to your privacy. Many people have been shocked to find out that the contents of their computer hard drive are available to the neighborhood cable network for all to see. If you have Windows networking engaged either unintentionally because that was the default out of the box, or you have a home LAN, then what you may not know is that sharing file access over a network is now (thanks to cable modem technology) visible to the world. It's something like the old-time party lines, where your neighbors could pick up their phones and listen in on your phone calls if they wanted to. Ensure that you take precautions if you have a computer connected in this manner. The "network sharing" option on your computer ought to be turned off if you don't really need it. And if you have any type of high-speed connection to the Internet, you have to become more serious about computer security. The law is still hazy on the issue, but conceivably a case could be made against you by a victim of a DoS attack launched using your computer system if it can be shown that you were neglectful in shielding your system from intruders.

How Did They Find You?

Computer scanning is not exactly something out of Dr. McCoy's medical station on *Star Trek,* but when it comes to finding out more about your computer it can be nearly as invasive. Scans often send signals that solicit an intelligent response from a computer. In this manner one can ascertain make, model, software versions, connectivity, ownership, and trust relationships.

Your computer can be overly helpful in volunteering this information. A certain amount of this type of activity is legitimate. It is required so computers can talk to each other or so that service providers can tailor the ways the information is presented. It is also required reconnaissance for threat agents like hackers and is often a precursor to more intrusive exploitation.

Scanning and probing begin innocently enough (undetectable below the noise level compared to regular traffic) before evolving into more provocative action. A light scan on a computer system is analogous in the real world to a thief driving by a parking lot to check out what cars are left unattended. An aggressive scan is like the thief checking the doors to see whether they are locked and looking inside the windows for valuables or alarm system indicators.

Scanning has become bolder and more widespread while at the same time masking much more sophisticated and potentially more serious stealth scanning activities. Security organizations around the world, including both the American and Canadian Computer Emergency Response Teams, have seen evidence of systematic network-vulnerability scanning of large domains. One such scan included all of Canada and everyone currently online. The U.S. Naval Surface Weapons Center has reported seeing multiple attackers using vulnerability scanning and stealth scanning techniques in a coordinated effort. The geographical dispersion of the attackers helps them avoid detection and capture

Obviously, the scanning process is highly automated. Turn your computer on and connect to the Internet . . . continue reading . . . by the time you finish reading this chapter your computer will be scanned. Stealth scanning can evade the attention of system administrators by probing the computers in a non-provocative manner over an extended period of time, gaining visibility into your world under the detection threshold of your firewalls or intrusion detection devices — casing your system one bit at a time. There's not much you can do to prevent this if you want to be connected to the Internet.

However, one countermeasure would be to get hold of a scanning program and scan your system yourself.

Falling into Software Holes

It seems everyone is in a hurry in the Internet world, and that includes the people making the software for e-mail and Web browsing. In the rush to keep up with the demand for more features, security questions sometimes go unanswered, until a resourceful hacker discovers a glitch that lets him sneak into your Web activities unnoticed. Security holes are found even on the newest Web browsers, soon after many of us have installed them on our systems. One such persistent glitch allows an attacker using Javascript "applets" (small software programs) to access the cache and history files, the cookie file and the hard disk structure on your computer. This means they can tell where you surfed and view any information you typed in to a form online. In early 2000, Netscape and Microsoft recommended that the Javascript capability be turned off until recent security holes had been fixed. No sooner had a patch been released for this vulnerability than another was announced. But how many of us have time to keep track of all these holes and security advisories, or to upgrade?

Major software companies have been criticized for selling products with underwhelming stability. Hackers see themselves as performing a vital role for the Internet community by discovering and publicizing holes in computer software, much like predators culling the weak from the herd. The altruistic gesture all too often crosses the line from vigilantism to crime.

If a hacker, or anyone else, discovers a security hole in a software program, the more prudent approach would be to quietly inform the makers of the program.

Announcing the discovery loudly and triumphantly in a public forum such as a newsgroup, as many "altruistic" hackers do, means that the vulnerability is known before a fix is available. A responsible software maker will scramble to devise a "patch" for the hole, but in the meantime users of the software, most of whom many not know of the problem or lack the ability to fix it themselves, are left open to attack.

Software bugs have always been a problem in the computer biz. There will be no solution until consumers become more vociferous and refuse to buy error-laden programs. Unfortunately, there will always be those keeners who must be the first on the block to have a new program, bugs and all. Software makers therefore have little incentive to improve their quality control procedures. In any case, for the average user, it is sometimes better to wait until the dust settles after a new release of software 1.0 and purchase the updated version 1.1.

Chapter 4
Agents of Chaos

Traditional classes of threat agents engaged in crime, espionage, and terrorism have been quick to adopt computers and the Internet for communications, propaganda, and intelligence gathering. Computer hackers have emerged as a new significant threat, and are predisposed to exploiting the technology for its own sake.

The threat to information systems does not stem exclusively from network exploitation; traditional methods such as extortion or the use of insider sources should also be considered. However, computers are one of the most cost-effective tools for attacking modern information systems, particularly when your network connections provide an existing conduit — your Internet connection. The networked nature of today's information systems and easy access to the Internet allow malicious attackers to remotely access systems from anywhere in the world. Not only does the Internet provide geographic remoteness, but it also affords a greater degree of anonymity, frustrating efforts to track down the perpetrator of an attack.

Threat Agents

Virtually anonymously they prowl interconnected networks, probing, scanning, and watching. They can attack and withdraw back into the ether at the speed of light. They are the hackers and crackers, telecommunications phreakers, precocious script kiddies, cyber-terrorists, and sophisticated organized crime operatives. Then, just when you think you know who they are, your business is blind-sided by one of your own employees with access to your most sensitive computer files.

Hackers simply enjoy the thrill of successfully breaking through technological barriers for its own sake and not necessarily to access information or acquire wealth. Most think of themselves as harmless pranksters. Despite their seemingly innocuous intentions, however, some hackers have emerged as a new significant threat to businesses. These are the cyber-vandals who wreak havoc just for the heck of it. The result of the attacks can be annoying, sometimes embarrassing and often costly. Terrorist and traditional criminals often have more sinister motives, but the results of their attacks may be the same as those by hackers. In the murky netherworld of cyberspace, the motives and intentions of hackers, crackers, phreakers, cyber-terrorists, and spies are difficult to determine at the best of times.

Who Are Hackers?

Here are some excepts from a "manifesto" written by a hacker known as "The Mentor." They offer some insight into the mentality of the hacker:

```
I am a hacker, enter my world . . .
    Mine is a world that begins with school
    . . . I'm smarter than most of the other
```

kids, this crap they teach us bores me . . .

I made a discovery today. I found a computer. Wait a second, this is cool. It does what I want it to. If it makes a mistake, it's because I screwed it up. Not because it doesn't like me . . .

Or feels threatened by me . . .

Or thinks I'm a smart ass . . .

Or doesn't like teaching and shouldn't be here . . .

And then it happened . . . a door opened to a world . . . rushing through the phone line like heroin through an addict's veins . . .

This is it . . . this is where I belong . . .

While they may seem to be a recent phenomenon, hackers have been around as long as computers. The term "hacker" originally referred to those software programmers who fiddled around with code in their spare time to remedy a sick program or to uncover new and interesting properties. Later their efforts were directed towards computer networks.

The meaning behind the word has become degraded since those days, as benign inquisitiveness on the part of the hacker has become corrupted, with more and more cases of malignant cyber attacks. Long gone is the idea of a cyberspace version of the "gentleman thief."

The glorification of hackers in the entertainment media has morphed the original meaning of the term into something significantly different. "We are used to seeing computer hackers portrayed in the media as youthful idealists who are simply engaged in a bit of mischievous fun. This did not match up with the reality of computer crime," commented the Australian Federal Minister of Justice in June 1999.

"Would you like to play a game? . . . How about Global Thermonuclear War?" This phrase is from the 1980 movie *War Games,* which is about a hacker who nearly ends life as we know it by penetrating the NORAD mainframe and inadvertently setting off a nuclear missile crisis. The look and feel of the movie was adopted by hacker culture. It served to glorify their activities and draw more players to the cause. Ira Winkler, author of *Corporate Espionage* and a former U.S. National Security Agency (NSA) employee, wrote, "After *War Games,* more and more teenagers started using their computers to access systems without permission.'

A decade later the theme was revamped by *Hackers,* a well-edited film that personified the hacking culture and introduced the catch phrase, "It is not who they are, it is what they do."

The mischievous side of hacking seems to have arisen from "phone phreaking" — the practice of breaking into telecommunications systems by technological means. Like hackers, phreakers were mostly motivate not by money but by the thrill of successfully breaking into a big corporation's system. The term "phracker" is sometimes used to describe those who hack both telecommunications and computer systems, but the convergence of telecommunications and computer systems has rendered the distinction between phreakers and phrackers largely academic.

The verb "hacking" has also become diluted to refer to all malicious activity occurring on computer networks. Conversely, anything or everything that a hacker does is referred to as "hacking." It has been said that when something means everything, it means nothing. The hacker identity is now also stricken with hypocrisy. In cyberspace, where identity and motive are obscured by anonymity, the agent for all deliberate threat events is "the hacker." There have been attempts to resuscitate the hacker name by disassociating "white hats" (good hackers with traditional values) from "black hats" (bad hackers or cyber-sociopaths) and labeling criminal hackers with the term "crackers," but for the mainstream media "hacker" remains the convenient catch-all term for anyone attacking a computer network or releasing a virus, regardless of motive. The white hats might be better off devoting their efforts to certifying themselves as "information technology security professionals." "Ethical hacker" has become an oxymoron.

Notwithstanding conflicts in terminology, any serious assessment of the threats to information systems needs to have an unequivocal definition of the hacker. For the purpose of this book you can think of a hacker as a person who exploits information technology for the sake of the technology. This distinguishes them from criminals, terrorists, or spies who may exploit a computer system using the same means but for entirely different motives — like stealing money or secrets.

Hacking is a rather meaningless term unless you stop to explain your interpretation at every juncture. In my work, I tend to replace the verb "hacking" with "network exploitation" or "computer exploitation," unless I am using it in the colloquial sense. I do not want the reader to get the impression that hackers (as in the popular culture group) are the only people who hack (break into computers).

Even where a definition of hacker can be agreed upon, there are different types of hackers. Hackers, crackers, and phreakers include those individuals or groups who are engaged in the exploitation of telecommunications, network and computer hosts. They are distinguished from other threat agents in that their prime objective is the use and abuse of this technology. Their activity is the most pervasive on the Internet. They prey on targets of opportunity rather than specific targets. Information gained is either used for other criminal purposes, or to further hacking activities. Motivation comes from the perceived cleverness and illustriousness of the hack. Inhibitions are eroded by the sense that a virtual crime is not a real crime. "Meta-crackers" represent more dangerous groups (organized crime or hostile intelligence services) and have been seen to prey upon lesser crackers and hackers. In the hacking community, things are often not what they seem.

At the top of the hacking food chain there are the "elite," groups such as the Cult of Dead Cow, L0pht Heavy Industries, Chaos Computer Club, Hong Kong Blondes, Legions of Doom, or individuals like John Draper (Cap'n Crunch), Kevin Mitnick, Kevin Poulsen, Robert Morris, the Datastream Cowboy, to mention a few. The elite lead the way in tools, tactics, and trends that eventually filter down to the average hacking group. Unlike the doings of novice hackers, elite activities usually go unnoticed except by the most discerning eyes. The Shadow Project run by the U.S. Naval Surface Warfare Center is one initiative designed to uncover the activities of the more sophisticated network intruders. Shadow recently uncovered widespread stealth scanning on U.S. government computer networks, underlining the point that what you can't see can still hurt you.

Hacktivism

Hacktivists are electronic guerrillas with political agendas ranging from ending censorship to outright sabotage. They have defaced government Web sites, toppled firewalls and even claimed to have disabled a satellite — although this was never proven to many people's satisfaction. In China and Mexico they demonstrated that they possess the tools to infiltrate government computer networks.

The concept of righteous hacking is in vogue. Participants stem from two sources: traditional crackers who view themselves as altruistic in otherwise illicit activities, and politically motivated activists who see hacking as a tool for advancing "the cause." As far as hacktivists are concerned, the Internet is not only rule-free and ethically liberal, but also serves as a large wall for political graffiti. There seems to be a general acceptance (at least within these spheres) that the end justifies the means.

One of the more reclusive hacktivist groups is the Toronto-based Hong Kong Blondes led by Blondie Wong, a dissident astrophysicist living in Toronto. The Blondes have led the way in "righteous hacking" and both the nuclear industry and non-democratic governments have been favorite targets. They have organized a virtual web of hackers to infiltrate the Chinese government networks, and to this end a splinter group was formed, known as the "Yellow Pages," which planned to target companies doing business with China, attacking their computer networks. The Hong Kong Blondes and the Yellow Pages draw support from several circles in areas where their agendas intersect, including a network of Chinese students, hacker groups, anarchists, electronic freedom supporters, and human rights groups. Some believe the Blondes do not really exist as a discrete group but rather as a loose coalition of many hacktivists sharing a common idea and name. The Blondes are on a first-name basis with the majority of elite hacking groups in the world, who have offered both tacit and tangible support to the Blondes' efforts, most notably the distribution of several thousand copies of the "Back Orifice" Trojan Horse program in China with the help of the Cult of the Dead Cow hacker group.

Cult of the Dead Cow (cDc) stated that "the Blondes have the capacity to snap the backbone of the Chinese end of the Net." It is believed the Hong Kong Blondes have been moderately successful in penetrating Chinese networks with the help of sympathizers in the Communist Party. Two members work out of Montreal, the alleged technical coordinator Lemon Li lives in Paris, while many members operate on the Chinese mainland — which can be perilous, if not life-threatening work. If hackers are caught in North America the authorities may terminate their account or in a few extreme cases put them in jail for a period of time, whereas the Chinese authorities have been known to execute hackers by firing squad.

Hacking groups have adopted social and political agendas since the beginning. The Chaos Computer Club has had several agendas in its lifetime and across the spectrum. This is how the Electronic Disturbance Theater, with acts of civil disobedience using techniques such as FloodNet — which causes a targeted Web site to constantly reload and thereby difficult to access — is able to successfully rationalize its activities and skirt the lines of the law. The truth is that most hackers are opportunists with one-day agendas and with a force of conviction traced along a compass heading influenced by the magnetic attraction of the moment. In this sense, many within the community view hackers as rebels without a cause, or at most, with one that is morally flexible.

Web Ethics

So, what are the ethical practices of cyberspace and how does society define hackers? As Dr. Gregory Walters, human rights professor at the University of Ottawa, explains, "the debate in society has not kept pace with technological evolution."

There is not a tenable linkage of moral acts and consequence between real and virtual worlds. Let me draw the introduction of the phone system as a parallel. Many people to this day talk to you differently on the telephone than in person. Messages left on voice mail are often poorly composed or terse. These are not the same standards for tone and language we would accept in a face-to-face encounter or in a written letter. How often have you received joke pornography in e-mail attachments from people who would not dare mail the same material to you in paper form? The extent of the problem can be seen in "Netiquette" advice columns, where a frequent question is how to politely decline these inappropriate and unwanted messages. Facing a computer screen than a human face can lead people do and say things on the Internet that they would never feel comfortable doing and saying in real life.

Unfortunately, actions and words uttered online become part of real life. I have seen, many a time, raunchy jokes circulate in an even wider distribution with the originating party's business signature blocks attached automatically by the e-mail application. How would this look for your company? It is very easy for people to share confidences online, but with one accidental click turn their private discussion into a public broadcast. I learned this the hard way when, in responding to an e-mail, I was lax with my language and tone; I felt I was talking among friends and did not care to take the time to choose my words carefully. One of the parties shared our conversation with the world by hitting the "Reply All" button and I spent the next week explaining myself. It only took this one incident for me to adopt the practice that anything I write in e-mails or I leave in messages on answering machines should be composed in such a manner that it could be broadcast without damaging my reputation or somebody else's.

Many hacker groups see it as morally acceptable to hack icons of evil in today's society. The hacker code-named Milw0rm hacked India's Bhabba Atomic Research Centre Web sites in protest against a nuclear test they had performed. Other purist hackers condemn actions such as Milw0rm's. The "bottom line is [that] conflicting moralities do not justify vigilante action," states an anonymous letter to Action-Online, commenting on hacking human rights abusers, polluters, and the nuclear industry. More often than not, hackers simply change their agenda so that they can hack with a clear conscience. For them, the hack is the thing.

On the other hand, assuming that all hackers are driven to pernicious ends by the "dark side of the force" and labeling them enemies of the state, is overly alarmist and erodes the credibility of the security community. Conveying a message through direct online action does not necessarily qualify as cyber-terrorism. It would not be the first time that the security intelligence apparatus chased a ghost of a cyber-spy ring only to find a 16-year-old high school student playing on his home computer at the other end of the line, with no agenda and few skills.

Script Kiddies

"Script kiddies," as these young hackers are known, are at the bottom of the hacking food chain. These are novices who have little understanding of computing and a tenuous grasp of Netiquette. They form the basis for the majority of the malicious activities occurring on the Internet today. Their modus operandi consists of downloading some of the many easy-to-use hacking programs off the Web, filling in a Web address, and pressing the launch attack button. The hacking programs are that simple to use. You no longer need to understand UNIX and TCP/IP-based networks, and be able to program in PERL to create serious mischief on the Net. Often the script kiddie becomes enamored with the new tool and like a kid who gets a new pellet gun for their birthday, shoots at everything in sight to see how it works. The targeting practices of the kiddie can be characterized as haphazard or opportunistic at best. Let us hope that your computer does not become a victim of chance.

The kiddies themselves are often preyed upon by meta-crackers or end up working unwittingly for organized crime syndicates, intelligence agencies, or at worst, terrorist groups. The opportunity to mount a false flag operation is ripe given the anonymity of cyberspace. A kid can think he is earning his badge towards elitism when in fact he is being manipulated by a state-sponsored terrorist group to harass an adversary. Sometimes they are just used as an unaware cut-out to pass information — an information "mule" trafficking contraband data. If someone catches on, guess who is going to take the fall?

This is no longer a hypothetical scenario. Harkat-ul-Ansar, a militant Indian separatist group, is on the U.S. State Department's list of the most dangerous terrorist organizations in the world. The group is closely aligned with Islamic militant Osama bin Laden. One evening last year an American teenager was using Internet relay chat (IRC — a worldwide, text-based network where real-world identities can be easily concealed) to boast about his hacking prowess when he was approached by an interested party named Ibrahim. The teen's new friend was after the Defense Information Systems Network Equipment Manager program. Ibrahim later sent the teen a $1000 U.S. money order for the military software. When the teenager could not produce the material, he found himself off Ibrahim's Xmas list and onto a Harkat-ul-Ansar hit list. At this point the FBI was called in by either the teen or his parents.

More recently, an unrepentant 16-year-old Montreal cracker and a member of "Groupe Segfault" became the center of an ongoing RCMP investigation for a wide campaign wreaking havoc on computer systems in Ontario, at the Massachusetts Institute of Technology and NASA, and Web sites associated with the RCMP, companies in Norway, the U.S. army, and various U.S. universities and government agencies. A Nova Scotia Internet service provider was assaulted electronically during the first three weeks of January 1999, using a type of denial of service attack. The RCMP is looking for a second accomplice in Nova Scotia.

We would disable Montreal in one second.
—Groupe Segfault, after their arrest

Getting Started

Parents, teachers, and anyone else responsible for the welfare of kids should be aware that it takes very little knowledge to do damage on the Internet. Combine this with the tendency of young people to view themselves as invincible and to not always think through the consequences of their actions, and you have the makings of an Internet disaster, with the incidents described above just a few examples.

In the last few years the number of web sites, electronic bulletin boards, chat rooms, and newsgroups dedicated to hacking has grown geometrically. There are now over 30,000 such places offering the latest in hacker "warez" (hacker slang for "hardware" or "software"). "I am really interested in hacking. Does anyone know of any cool free software?" is a typical posting by a newbie on the alt.2600 hacker newsgroup. This is how script kiddies begin their travels on the slippery slope that nearly always leads to getting caught.

The tools of illicit hacker activities are readily available to anyone who wants them. To prove this point to a client, a friend of mine downloaded over 4,000 hacking exploits off the Net that did everything from break and enter to snoop and destroy. It took two nights to download them, then he burned them onto a CD-ROM. Voila! A turnkey information warfare capability at almost no cost. To see just how easy this is, go to a search engine like www.altavista.com, type in a search for the keywords "hacker exploits software," and see where it gets you.

> *WARNING!* Do not download or use whatever you find. You may get more than you bargained for — a nasty virus, or a knock on your door from the authorities!

"A monkey could hack a computer," says Ira Winkler, author of Corporate Espionage and former National Security Agency (NSA) employee. "It is easy to break into computers, the hard part is to protect them."

What Do Hackers Do?

Hackers do not see themselves as evil or their activities as malicious. Most really believe they're just out for a bit of harmless fun. Some even claim their work is beneficial to society, because they often discover security gaps in the Net that could be exploited by the real bad guys. To them, what they do is like breaking into your car and leaving you a note telling you to get an alarm.

Recently, a government supercomputer was turned into one of the most popular worldwide hacker chat servers by some hacking group. It became a victim of its own success when the sheer volume of traffic crashed wide area networks, thereby drawing the attention of the authorities. Control of the site was then quietly re-assumed by the government, who monitored the major-ity of global hacker chat traffic for a period. The problem for the authorities was that the channels were void of intelligent conversations. Sifting through tens of thou-sands of conversations for something worthwhile was akin to looking for a needle in a haystack and was sim-ply not cost effective. The site was subsequently shut down and the supercomputer patched up. Big computers are always big targets.

It might be argued that in this instance hackers did find a potentially dangerous exposure in an important computer system. But many other cases could be cited in which hacker antics have had very real, detrimental effects. One example: Police and emergency crews responded time and time again to tornado warning sirens that sounded in rural Kentucky throughout the month of October 1999. Apparently, someone had mim-icked the activation tones by hacking into the system.

Truth and Consequences: The Case of the Phonemasters

The line between hacker and criminal — or "cracker" — can be very fine, as you will see in the following true story. The Phonemasters were phrackers, a mixture of phone phreakers and hackers who initially met in the murky world of underground bulletin boards and marauded through telecommunications circuits and computers. The extent of their escapades is only now coming to light.

Eleven people barely in their twenties were accused of the "most extensive illegal breach of the nation's telecommunications infrastructure in high tech history," reported the *Wall Street Journal,* on October 1, 1999. Three members ended up serving time in prison, while the rest are likely online somewhere.

Some of their activities could be attributed to a wry sense of humor at the expense of law enforcement agencies, like the time they made the Pennsylvania Police Department phone number appear on thousands of pagers across the country at the same time. The influx of calls swamped the station. Or the time the FBI received a $200,000 phone bill because FBI field office numbers had been forwarded to sex-chat lines in Germany, Hong Kong, and Moldavia. Or maybe the time the Phonemasters hacked into the U.S. West Bell Telephone database, obtained a list of telephone numbers under surveillance by police, and called a drug dealer on the list to leak the news to him, just for the hell of it.

Then there were actions committed out of inquisitiveness. One day the group discovered unpublished White House numbers by breaking into Mrs. Clinton's (senior) telephone billing records in Arkansas, and then called a few. The Phonemasters would eavesdrop and redirect phone calls for fun.

However, much of their lives as phrackers took on a sinister and profiteering trend. The group gained access to the networks of AT&T Corp., British Telecom Inc., GTE Corp., MCI WorldCom, SouthWestern Bell, and Sprint Corp. They penetrated the credit reporting databases of Equifax Inc., and TRW Inc., compromised the Nexis/Lexis databases and those of Dun & Bradstreet. The Phonemasters went on to access portions of the national power grid and air-traffic control systems.

Not all of their exploits involved hacking. Frequently, some of them resorted to Dumpster diving (going through garbage), and social engineering (telephone fraud) so as to steal passwords. "Fraud is a beautiful thing," a group member stated, captured on tape by the FBI.

Altogether they were accused of misusing, abusing, and netting $1.8 million in materials and services. It is difficult to know for certain what costs were incurred or how much damage was actually caused by the group's activities. They sold information to organized crime figures, private investigators, and information brokers. One heist from Sprint netted nearly 1000 calling card access codes that were transferred to a man in Canada who paid $17,000 for them. The codes ended up in the hands of a Sicilian Mafia operative in Switzerland.

A Texas private investigator tipped off the FBI to the existence of the group. A member of the Phonemasters had solicited the P.I. with a shopping list for personal credit reports, motor vehicle records, Police Crime Information Center records, and unlisted phone numbers. The FBI placed a dial number recorder tap on the member's phone line and captured the phone numbers of incoming and outgoing calls. Traffic analysis on the phone records revealed some interesting patterns. He was online 15 hours a day, connected to every major telecommunications carrier in the country; some of the calls even included unlisted numbers at the White House. All of this was occurring from his room in his parents' home.

Based upon these calling patterns, the FBI justified installing a digital wire tap on the subscriber line exiting the home, which would pick up the dialed number information and voice calls, and most important, demodulate the modem signals. The subsequent unfiltered data were overwhelming. The mounting evidence would eventually fill a twenty-square-foot room.

This member of the Phonemasters was to be informed by his conspirators that his number had appeared on their lists as being monitored by the FBI.

Soon afterwards, there was a knock at the door. It was noted in court statements that despite the walls of the room being plastered with phone numbers, the parents were in denial. On a tape that was entered into evidence in court, the Phonemasters could be heard saying, "Do you know how ironic that's gonna be when they play those tapes in court? . . . and they got you saying it was the FBI tapping in?"

Cyber-Criminals

Hackers and phrackers, according to our definition, do not view themselves as criminals, even if their actions result in major financial losses to their targets. They do not acknowledge that charging their online activities to someone else's phone accounts is theft. Like the Phonemasters, some hackers find they need to steal in order to continue their hacking activity. After all, someone has to pay for their equipment and phone lines. Thus, there is a bit of a gray area when distinguishing hackers from criminals, but for our purposes true cyber-criminals set out to steal from the very beginning. They aren't intrude on private computer networks for fun. Petty or organized cyber-criminal activities are motivated by the acquisition of money and power. For example, Russian crime groups have a high level of sophistication, especially in the area of electronic commerce, money laundering, extortion, drug trafficking and smuggling. This type of criminal is typically well educated and well connected. Many were involved in the security services of the former Soviet Union. It is rumored that the Russian "Mafia" has taken control of 80 per cent of all Russian commercial enterprises, particularly targeting the financial sector. Any serious investigation has been frustrated by a lack of real access. Most of the 2,000 banks in Russia appear to be controlled by organized crime.

Russian organized crime groups have been quick to go online. The European Union Bank, operated out of Toronto and the first Internet bank in the world, allegedly was a front for the Russian Mafia. A Russian Web site provides software to crack the licenses of 71 commercial products, including the most widely used personal firewall. Motorcycle gangs too have discovered the Web: members have been seen attending Internet security courses offered by the police. It is predicted by many in the security profession that transnational and domestic crime groups will emerge as a serious threat as government and industry move to implement e-commerce.

Cybotage

Just as traditional criminals have added the Internet to their toolbox, political extremists have also found it a useful means for promoting their agendas. Cybotage is sabotage from cyberspace, and its effects cross the boundary between virtual and real worlds. Sabotage of telecommunication and information systems is nothing new. It has occurred within Canada and the U.S. and has included a range of disruptive activities, such as the bombing of microwave towers a decade ago. Localized acts of network-spawned sabotage have also been felt. On March 10, 1997, a threat agent in Massachusetts knocked out power at the Worcester airport, disrupting communications between aircraft and the control tower for six hours. This type of attack is particularly difficult to deal with because it often manifests itself in system errors, such as slow execution of procedures and misdirection of information, that could be easily attributed to accidental technical malfunctions.

Where formerly a saboteur would need physical access to disrupt a vital system — to cut cables, drop poison in a water system, or place a bomb in a transformer station — the Internet now provides a conduit that can be used at a safe geographical distance to produce similarly disruptive results. And as we become more reliant on the Internet for communications and financial activities, the Internet itself will become a target. In an interesting combination of the old and the new, a trans-American fiber cable was physically severed in 1998, shutting down the Internet in major areas of the U.S.

Cybotage is another area in which the boundaries between the hacker and the malevolent attacker blur. The results of their activities may be the same, but their intents may not be. The hacker may be an over-reaching adolescent trying to impress his friends, with little regard for the consequences. The saboteur, however, is quite intent on the consequences of knocking out vital systems. That a young hacker can perpetrate the same results shows the vulnerability of our infrastructure to hostile forces. In fact, as shown in an earlier example, the Internet not only offers the means to launch an attack, but also a great tool for recruiting the naïve hacker who has the skills those with sinister motives need to do the job.

Cyber-Terrorism

There are many things trolling the Internet far worse than hackers. Terrorist groups have displayed the ability to attack a target's financial, operational, and information base electronically. The Internet has expanded and magnified the threats posed by these groups, due to the capabilities it affords them: rapid and encrypted communications, anonymity, remote operations, direct action, and information gathering without having a physical presence. Network exploitation is a means to an end and a growing weapon in the terrorist's arsenal.

The Internet also provides the capability to disseminate propaganda and recruit members with valuable skills or access. Some of these groups network with the hacker community for the purpose of exchanging operational ideas.

Cyber-terrorists are plotting all manner of heinous attacks that, if successful, could "destabilize and eventually destroy targeted states and societies. Information warfare specialists estimate that a properly prepared and well-coordinated attack by fewer than 30 computer virtuosos or cyber-terrorist groups strategically located around the world, with a budget of less than $10 million, would shut down everything from electric power grids to air traffic control centers," according to a gloomy report from the Center for Strategic and International Studies (CSIS).

The accepted premise amongst security experts is that the use of cyberspace as a terrorist weapon is predicated upon the development and proliferation of state-sponsored information warfare operations. To date countries have been reluctant to use offensive information capabilities owing to fear of retaliation and unfamiliarity with the technology at the political levels. Yet, according to an interesting 1999 report by the RAND corporation entitled, "Countering the New Terrorism," we can expect to see a rise in state-sponsored terrorism in the modern age post-2000. Terrorists, they observed, move in loose groups, constellations with free-flowing structures (segmented, polycentric, ideologically integrated) that map ideally to the technologies and culture of cyberspace.

Spy vs. Spy

Intelligence is the business of collecting, processing, and reporting information. The majority of the world's information is stored on or communicated by computers. It stands to reason that if you were a spy, that is where you would have to look. Or get someone to look for you.

Governments, including our own, have been at this for quite a while. The Internet is merely another intelligence-gathering tool. The European Parliament has raised concerns about ECHELON, a surveillance web controlled by an alliance of the U.S., Canada, Britain, Australia and New Zealand. There is not a lot of public information about this rather shadowy alliance, but former employees of various government security agencies say ECHELON nations cooperate in sharing intercepted phone calls, faxes and e-mails. The European Parliament report on the system claimed that it was being used not only for anti-terrorism and other national security efforts, but also for industrial espionage.

The Russian Federal Agency for Government Communications (FAPSI) is part of the Russian Security Service (FSB) — the successor to the beloved KGB. You will also be happy to know that FAPSI and the FSB have joined forces to control Relcom, the largest computer Internet service provider in Russia. On the books is a not-so-secret project, code-named STORMII, which is intended to rein in all the independent Internet service providers into the agencies' data collection efforts by installing data intercept devices at all major network points.

What makes such efforts particularly worrisome is the way in which the line between state security services and crime organizations is sometimes blurred, as is the distinction between patriots and zealots.

"We use computers to send viruses to the West," boasted Russian ultra-nationalist, Vladimir Zhirinovsky, "and then we poach your money."

The Russians have taken an aggressive and bold approach to their intelligence-gathering practices. These are seen in direct contrast to their traditional human source methods, which have been characterized as cautious. Lengthy investigations have uncovered a tangled web of intrigue and skullduggery involving America's former cold war antagonist. In an operation known as Moonlight Maze, U.S. authorities discovered that secrets were being purloined from defense computers involving weapon guidance systems and naval intelligence codes. The attack assessment by the U.S. government is predictably grim. The deputy defense secretary in a congressional hearing stated in no uncertain terms that "we are in the middle of a cyberwar."

Many of the attacks were traced to Moscow and the Academy of Sciences, but the Kremlin may not be the culprit. There has been speculation within the professional security community that part of the activities could be attributed to organized crime operating as a front for the security service.

"There were deliberate and highly co-ordinated attacks occurring in our defense department that appear to be coming from one country . . . it is very real and very alarming," said Curt Weldon, chairman of a congressional committee for research and development. To date, cooperation by the Russian government in resolving these incidents has been underwhelming.

Information Warfare

I have been in the information warfare business for the majority of my adult life and did not know it. This is because the term "information warfare" (IW), or the politically correct term "information operations" (IO), came into usage in the early nineties. IO has grown to include all aspects of military operations to degrade or destroy the information and systems of an adversary while protecting your own. IO has both offensive and defensive thrusts that cannot exist without each other. Categories within IO include electronic warfare (jamming, radio direction, finding, interception of both communications and radar), signals and electronic intelligence (spy satellites to listening posts), network exploitation (state-sponsored hacking), psychological operations (propaganda and deception), all manner of intelligence gathering, reconnaissance, and information technology security, and many more fields dealing with information protection or exploitation. It was recognized very early that information warfare would benefit from the synergy of related information disciplines. Together, they act as a force multiplier.

In the last two decades we have experienced a convergence of technologies in which electronics, telecommunications, broadcasting, and computing are becoming one. At the center are computers and networks. Military operations must evolve with the times. Not only is modern weaponry like jets, smart bombs, navigational systems, mobile communications systems and optical systems becoming highly dependent upon computing technology, but the prized assets that our adversary is trying to protect are also computer driven. Surprisingly, many of these opposing weapon systems and assets are tied together in cyberspace.

During the Kosovo conflict, for example, one of the most successful means of delivering munitions to a target, such as a Serb headquarters, was to use smart bombs guided by the Global Positioning System (GPS). The GPS uses constellations of satellites orbiting the

Earth to transmit signals to the receiver (in this case the smart bomb) which uses the data to calculate a position in three dimensional space plus time. The signals are accurate to less than a meter in position and 100 nanoseconds in time.

Precise time is the key to making the system work. Time is kept within one microsecond of Coordinated Universal Time by the U.S. Naval Observatory. GPS time is a composite time derived from atomic clocks at all terrestrial monitoring stations and onboard all the satellites. The clocks at the terrestrial stations around the world in turn synchronize with each other and with the satellites to give National Time Standards.

Defining correct time on Earth is an iterative and cooperative process amongst nations that occurs over the Internet. This same time is used to synchronize computer networks across the world, including those at the Serbian headquarters being bombed. Theoretically, you can trace a path from the smart bomb's navigational system through the Internet to the Serb HQ computers. In practice, subverting the path of the bomb from a PC on the desk of some Serb soldier is a non-trivial task. A better way is to jam the GPS signal that the bomb's receiver needs to acquire to hit the target. This falls into the field of Information Operations/class: Electronic Warfare/sub-class: Electronic Counter Measures/Sub-subclass: Communications Jamming.

All this James Bond–like activity may not seem to have much to do with the security of your home or business computer systems, and in fact, you are unlikely to be directly targeted, but you may be indirectly affected. Attacks using information systems are not always directed at system components, but also seek to affect and exploit the trust users have in the integrity and validity of the information in them. As we rely more and more on the Internet for communications and commercial transactions, the threat to the infrastructure they depend on could have serious economic repercussions.

Furthermore, the difference between war making of the past and today is that the Internet now enables all players to get into the game with the big boys on nearly an equal footing. Cyberspace technology has invoked the concept of "asymmetrical" threats. This term refers to weapons and tactics that empower groups of modest means to successfully engage a much larger target, such as a government. Given today's infrastructure, a hostile group need not destroy large portions of the infrastructure to be effective.

The irony is that the ability for a traditional superpower to strike back at a terrorist cell is limited in that this cell has little computing infrastructure that can be counter-attacked. Conversely, most Western countries have sprawling information infrastructures that are perforated with exposures. The risk to our infrastructure is largely contingent upon the motives of these various threat agents, and there is a great deal of uncertainty associated with intent.

Not only can small groups wreak havoc on an adversary's communications through the Internet, it can use the Internet very effectively for propaganda purposes. During the conflict in Yugoslavia a Serbian para-military group pumped out propaganda through newsgroup postings on the Internet, in which they encouraged expatriates to become politically active. They also operated several state-sponsored pro-Serbian Web sites. The Web sites were primarily established in response to western news media and to counter-act the Kosovo Liberation Army Web site that had been running for several years, and the Radio B92 Belgrade alternative media outlet mirrored in Netherlands.

One of the more annoying things that the Serbs did was to spam millions of American, Canadian, and British citizens directly with e-mail propaganda. In a bolder move, a stream of viruses and denial of service attacks were cast on NATO Web sites. The U.S. Air Force issued a warning to troops to refrain from surfing to former Yugoslavian Web sites, as doing so might give the site operators hints about what their command was interested in.

When the harassment became bothersome and the communication channel into Yugoslavia was no longer required by NATO, the Americans severed Yugoslavia's connection to cyberspace. This action was a double-edged sword in that the U.S. could no longer mount offensive network attacks of its own over these channels.

The Enemy Within

For all this discussion of anonymous foreigners out to do our computers harm, often the real threat is right under our noses. We have seen the damage an inquisitive teenager can do with a computer, which should impress on parents and teachers the need to supervise young people's computer activities. Similar vigilance needs to be deployed in the workplace as well. With networked computer access, employees can directly affect the well being of the enterprise, whether governmental or commercial. There is a potential exposure to the actions of a disgruntled employee, a criminal, or a subverted or recruited individual. Actions may include theft, bribery, graft, extortion, breach of trust, or willful damage (DoS attack). The threat potential will depend upon a variety of factors, including intentions, access, skills, opportunity, means, motivation, and payoff.

The insider threat to computer systems varies slightly from traditional damage. As a matter of doing business the employer must give their employees some access to the corporate computer network. Access privileges are granted on the basis of trust or better yet, trustworthiness. Unfortunately, vetting the employee's résumé is likely the only input into an employer's trust decision. Computer protective measures and monitoring systems are usually only adequate enough to keep the honest people out. The insider, therefore, often has much greater access than they strictly require, giving them the capacity to seriously affect system operations or the information contained therein on a wide scale. Deleting all the company files may be as destructive as burning the building down. The Internet allows for a communication path for traditional crime. White-collar crime is aided by the Internet, particularly as it extends into your business. An insider can push sensitive information out of your site using your own Internet connections.

An even more subtle crime is theft of information. A precise electronic copy of a computer file can be made without necessarily affecting the original. The thief does not have to remove the original material nor is the owner left without their copy. Much like using the old-fashioned photocopier, the document's owner is none the wiser. Once again, this illustrates that the value lies in the information, not the paper or electrons.

Since simple possession of information is not a crime (at least not yet), the transgression occurs in the manner in which it was obtained and used. It is therefore imperative that the thief is either caught in the act of illicitly accessing the file or nabbed later trying to profit from it.

Chapter 5
Playing Out of Bounds

The best way to attack a computer is with a computer. But even for hackers who consider hacking as an end unto itself the virtual world cannot always provide the needed access to your information and computer power. When this situation arises, they join traditional criminals and default to real life (RL) antics and deceit, which they veneer with new terms like "social engineering" and "Dumpster diving."

Threat agents have several preferred means of acquiring information when your online security is too good. In regards to Internet security, the data they seek are usually passwords and other information necessary to continue to exploit your computer through the Internet.

Hacking Wetware:
Social Engineering Ploys

"Wetware" — in contrast to software or hardware — refers to the human mind. Gathering intelligence from humans by nefarious means is nothing new. In fact "it is the second oldest profession, and just about as honorable as the first." Even with new hacker tools appearing on the Net every week, exploiting human naïveté will remain one of the most effective means of subjugating network security. Hoodwinking users over the phone is referred to delightfully as "social engineering," and it is clearly not hacking. What it is is good old-fashioned fraud. Social engineering as defined in the hacker glossary is the art of manipulating and deceiving people to perform actions that more greatly expose the computer systems of a network. It does serve the same purpose as hacking, however — gaining access, control, and more access. It is much easier to simply ask users for their password than to break into a computer and retrieve it.

The goal of most social engineering is to persuade legitimate users of your computer network to give up their password. This is usually done over the telephone or through e-mail. A common tactic is for the bad guy to masquerade as an authority figure such as a system administrator, service provider, or telecommunications technician. The victim would get a call out of the blue requesting some vital information to fix a computer problem. The reasoning is specious and fraught with techno jargon. The tactic works all too often. With this in mind, staff should be instructed never to give their password to anyone.

Other than the phone-call-out-of-the-blue-for-your-password trick, hackers will perform triage of the target site using subtler ploys. The company phone directory and organization chart is a good place to start. In order to sound convincing it is useful to drop some name into a conversation — "Bob asked me to check with Karen in marketing about . . . " The more the bad guys know about an organization, the more legitimate they will seem in these conversations. They want to know what type of computer hardware and software you are using. They may ask you if there are any modems connected to any of the computers and request the dial-up numbers associated with those connections (perhaps written right on the modem). In the case of many networked computers, all the intruder may need to gain access is to get you to reboot your machine. Hackers, as one example, may try and convince you to install a piece of software containing a Trojan horse program. It may be called an "enhancement," an "upgrade" or a "security patch." A real system administrator already has access to your computer to make these changes and would never ask users to do this themselves.

Social engineering often also extends to hacker exploits themselves. The "I love You" and "Melissa" virus-worm-Trojan packages, for instance, were wrapped and delivered using the same understanding of psychology. Few could resist the lure of the subject lines of the e-mails carrying these nasty surprises. This social engineering ploy was largely responsible for the success of these malicious programs, which were not all that sophisticated from a technical standpoint.

Dumpster Diving

Pseudo-hacking can be a dirty business. One person's trash is another's treasure, and sometimes information remains valuable long after it is discarded. So it is with hackers who dive into garbage bins outside of commercial establishments looking for anything that could be helpful in sustaining or advancing their hacking cause.

Dumpster diving is a means to an end. It is not very glorious, it is not hacking, and in many places it is illegal. The question of who owns your trash has been taken up in a number of court cases. In general, it has been determined that items in garbage receptacles on private property remain private property. If the receptacle is placed on public property, such as the curbside, it's a matter of "finders keepers."

In any case, some thought should be given to how your sensitive documents will be disposed of. The range of items to be considered may surprise you: technical manuals, internal phone books, journals with passwords written on them — all are useful in casing the corporate network for either direct network exploitation or for scripting an identity (a "legend") for social engineering purposes. It also goes beyond paper; remember when you throw that diskette out that even if you deleted the contents, the information can still be retrieved through a process called "media reconstruction." Even hard disks that have been damaged by fire and water can be salvaged with today's technology at a cost. The deleted company memos on discarded diskettes may be reconstructed by an average hacker using off-the-shelf utilities.

Larger companies with customer databases and industrial secrets to protect may seem the only likely targets worth digging through stinky garbage for, but not all Dumpster divers are looking for information tidbits to sell. Hackers need Internet accounts, access, and computers to do their work, and these all cost money. So credit card receipts, bank accounts, checks, and other financial information can be useful in purchasing what they need online. A few years ago in Ottawa, Canada, I had supper at a downtown cafe that I knew was frequented by hacker groups. We could see and hear a meeting as it took place adjacent to us. In a word "uninteresting." We finished up, paid the waitress and thought nothing more of it. That is until my VISA bill came in three weeks later. There were several thousand dollars of illicit purchases from locations across Europe and North America. Most of the purchases were for computer-related stuff. It turned out that some of the hackers after their meeting had stolen credit card receipts from the cafe's garbage, or en route to the Dumpster. I had ripped my receipt up, so they had to have pieced it back together.

The same individuals posted the credit card numbers on the Internet claiming that they had obtained the information by hacking into VISA's mainframe. Although we know who sold the credit card numbers and posted them, there was not enough evidence to convict. However, the interesting thing was that the fraudulent credit card purchases all involved goods that were shipped to a physical, real-world address and a door that the authorities were able to knock on. One of the fraudulent charges made on my card was for an Internet account. I was able to contact the provider, who placed a watch on the user's activities. Then it was over to VISA security and the law enforcement agency to trace the number and recover the charges.

By the way, I do not leave credit card receipts, even ripped up, at restaurants anymore.

Onsite Tactics

When social engineering by phone or e-mail and Dumpster diving won't do the trick, desperate threat agents may take the next step and bring themselves bodily to your place of business to try to persuade you or your employees to give them the information they need. The bolder among them will use the same types of social engineering ploys in person that they used on the phone.

And sometimes you will welcome them with open arms. In a variation on the social engineering theme, some threat agents apparently used the panic about the Y2K bug in 1999 to gain a foot in the door of a number of companies and organizations. The dire predictions of what would transpire on January 1, 2000, when computers and software designed with apparently little forethought were unprepared to accept "00" as a date, did not come to pass. Few disruptions were reported and no one was forced to retreat to their bunker.

But the Y2K bug may yet have a nasty impact. The greater threat to the security of many systems may not have been the bug itself, but rather the hasty efforts undertaken to address the issue. Fixing the Y2K problem turned into a billion-dollar industry with critical timelines. Security measures became secondary. In some cases unvetted individuals were given access to critical systems to get the job done quickly. Some commercial and public enterprises have found malicious code such as trap doors and Trojans implanted in their computer systems by contractors during the course of Y2K work. Others have found that the confidentiality and integrity of their corporate information was compromised.

In the case of the Y2K bug, the cure may yet turn out to be worse than the disease. Other ploys are not so elaborate. Hackers have been known to masquerade as cleaners, bike couriers, plant tenders, building staff, phone repair technicians, hydro workers, new employees, and clients, to name a few. They are on an intelligence-gathering mission of sorts — anything that will give them additional access. They wander around the office unnoticed or ignored, looking for an untended computer. It takes less than 30 seconds for a skilled cyber-thief to steal a password from a computer. While you're on your coffee break or off doing some photocopying, they can re-boot your machine and bypass security at start-up or they can install a sniffer on your hard drive.

Sometimes they don't even need to touch your computer. They can simply peer over your shoulder as you type in your password ("shoulder surfing") or read it from the note you've stuck to your keyboard or from where you wrote it on your desk blotter or . . . you get the idea. Computers left on with no screen-saver password are simply too tempting to pass up. With today's Web cameras on computers, it may be possible for someone to watch you remotely. How many companies have the screens of the computers visible through the outside window or from the office tower across the street? It can be easier for someone to spy on you with a telescope to get your password than to try and hack in.

Steal the Computer

If it is the information you are after and the computer is small enough, why not just steal it? The portability of laptop computers has made them very popular for business travelers and telecommuters. It also makes them popular targets of thieves. Intel estimates that over 300,000 laptop computers were stolen in 1999. The machine itself is worth between $5,000 and $15,000. As a bonus, thieves are learning, the information it contains can be worth much more. Take the example of the Gulf War plans for the ground invasion that were stored on a laptop stolen from the trunk of a car in London, England.

Be very suspicious of a theft in the office where easy-to-access computers have been passed over and one computer singled out. This is reason to suspect that it was the information on that particular machine that was targeted, not the computer hardware itself. One such case involved industrial espionage within a high-tech company in "Silicon Valley North" in Kanata, Ontario. An engineer had his laptop stolen from within the offices of a rival company he was visiting.

Physical Attack

When a network denial of service attack fails to bring a company to its knees, a threat agent can resort to breaking things. This is perhaps taking hacking to the extreme. Unfortunately, it is all too common. Critical infrastructures such as pipelines, telecommunications wires, and bridges have fallen prey to this sort of direct action. Consider the following example: July 13, 1997, has been characterized as the worst day of the worst week in the history of the Internet. The data communications backbone was severed, paralyzing traffic. The disruption was caused by the cutting of a cross-continent fiber optic cable. Nothing to do with hacking, except the attack was planned and organized online by people previously known as hackers. A total of 1559 DS-3s (really big communications pipes) were taken down in two days, effectively shutting down the North American Internet for that period.

More exotic approaches to physical attack are being developed. How about bombarding your computer with high energy? An attacker could theoretically send high voltage pulses through your phone line or a powerful photonic blast down the fiber and fry your systems. High-energy radio frequency and electromagnetic pulse guns gave been conceived and tested in the laboratory. But for the average citizen, being attacked in this manner is not likely. High pay-off targets haven't been as lucky — the victim in one heist was a bank alarm system.

Chapter 6
The Sorcerer's Apprentice: Exploits and Trade Craft

*P*erhaps the most foreboding place on Earth is of our own design. In this world, there is a pandemic of malicious code and diabolical devices bounded only by the imagination of their creators. More disquieting is the knowledge that the architects have lost control of some of their more damaging creations, allowing stealth-polymorphic viruses, intelligence software agents and other scary-sounding things to propagate over the Internet unchecked. Knowing something about the technical tools and methods used by threat agents to attack your computer system will help you to determine what sorts of security measures and devices you need to employ.

Twenty new exploits are released on the Internet every month. Powerful and potentially damaging software devices are so easy to acquire for free off the Internet that they are in reach of even the most apathetic hacker. If you know your fairy tales, you know what happens when the incompetent get hold of powerful devices. In case you don't, here's one story.

The Sorcerer's Apprentice

It started out as a perfectly normal day for a sorcerer's apprentice. He began daydreaming as usual about obtaining magical powers. Normal, that is, until he found the Sorcerer's wand left unattended in the spell room. The apprentice enchanted a legion of helpers to fill the tub, sank comfortably into the sorcerer's chair, and fell quietly asleep. The dream turned into a nightmare and that into reality as he awoke to find that the helpers had turned the Sorcerer's cavern into a subterranean sea!

This story parallels the experimentation of novice hackers — the "script kiddies" described in chapter 4 — with powerful exploits which they do not fully understand, cannot control, and of which they rarely foresee the potentially damaging outcome.

The proverbial sorcerer's spell room had been left unattended and accessible from the Internet. Any of us can access potions, incantations and magical devices beyond our comprehension and sometimes beyond our ability to control.

Potions: Malicious Code

We can look upon malicious code — nasty software — as being like the sorcerer's potions sitting on the laboratory shelf. All it takes is someone to come along and pour the contents into the well. The greatest threat originates from programs that are designed to operate independently of their creator, with the intent and potential to harm system components. At one time, harmful code, such as a virus would be introduced into computer systems by means of removable media such as infected diskettes and CD-ROMs. Now this malicious software can spread pervasively through Internet and network connections. A few isolated cases can quickly turn into a pandemic.

Malicious code can take a variety of forms, the names of which are drawn from the similarities they share with real-world pathogens. The one most people can identify with is the computer virus.

Viruses

According to an *Information Week* survey published in July 1999, 64 per cent of companies had fallen victim to a virus attack in the previous year. The International Computer Security Association's computer virus prevalence survey showed that computer viruses doubled every year from 1997 to 1999.

Computer viruses, like their real world cousins, can copy themselves. Viruses need your computer as a host in which to live. They use up system resources and frequently perform harmful functions. They are designed to be highly contagious and to propagate through computer systems.

Computer viruses do not occur naturally in cyberspace. They are man-made. The image springs to mind of mad scientists brewing up viruses in some level four biohazard lab, or the nasty things escaping from an ultra-secret military biological weapons facility. But in truth, most computer viruses are written by hobbyists and released by the less savory.

A whole industry has grown up around viruses and providing protection from them. Sometimes they leak out of legitimate research establishments, or are deliberately set upon adversaries by warring factions. Chances are that if you catch a computer virus, the culprit will be either a hooligan deliberately targeting your system or a close friend unknowingly acting as a carrier by sending you an infected diskette or e-mail attachment.

Trojan Horses

The Trojan Horse in Greek legend was a large, hollow wooden horse in which the attacking Greek troops hid. It was presented to the Trojans as an offering to the goddess Athena. Accordingly, the Trojans hauled the horse into their fortified city. In this way their enemies the Greeks were able to gain entrance into and capture the city of Troy, thus ending the Trojan War.

Similarly, a Trojan horse program is software that, in addition to appearing to operate as expected, has a hidden function that does something much more. This extra function is almost always damaging.

Powerful exploitation tools such as "Back Orifice" and "Netbus" are most often hidden in software as Trojan horses. Both Back Orifice and Netbus function as self-contained, self-installing utilities that allow the perpetrator to remotely control and monitor computers running the Windows operating system over a network. When the host program is run by the target system, a Trojan horse is installed on the hard drive that permits total control of the targeted system. Even more distressing is the fact that older versions of virus-scanning software do not detect Trojan horses.

Droppers, Logic Bombs and Worms

The manner in which the poisons and potions of cyberspace are administered is as interesting as it is alarming. Here are few ways in which they are deployed:

Droppers act as carriers for viruses, like rats carrying the plague. These programs install a virus into memory, onto the disk, or into a file.

Logic bombs are programs that wait in memory for a specific trigger such as a date or a series of conditions before executing. Like a timer on a fuse, they allow the guilty to retreat to a safe distance and time before their actions have an effect. Often the gestation period of a viral infection can be engineered to permit the maximum number of computers to be infected. After all, if the lethality of the virus were quick and complete, it would kill its host before it could infect other systems.

Worms are virus-like programs that use network connections to propagate and infect other systems.

Concoctions

If you took all the bottles on the sorcerer's shelves and mixed the contents, the resultant concoction would pack quite a punch. Lately we have begun to see a convergence of malicious code types into virus-worm-Trojan hybrids. The most harmful properties of each type — the simplicity of viruses, the pervasiveness of worms, and the control of Trojans — combine to produce a powerful impact.

Since the summer of 1999, the CERT Coordination Center at Carnegie Mellon University has issued three urgent advisories involving malicious code. All these viruses-worms-Trojans have had a negative impact on computer users around the world:

» *ExplorerZip Trojan* — During the second week of June 1999, this Trojan horse-worm program, propagated through e-mail attachments, began damaging Windows-based systems. Explorer.zip.exe created havoc in the computer e-mail systems of Microsoft, Intel, and NBC.

» *Chernobyl Virus* — this virus became active on April 26, 1999, the 13th anniversary of the Chernobyl nuclear plant disaster. It seems set to reactivate every year on that date. It has not been widespread so far, but it can have a serious impact, as it attempts to erase a computer's hard drive.

» *Melissa Macro Virus* — The Microsoft Word 97 and Word 2000 macro virus propagated through e-mail attachments beginning on March 26, 1999. The number and variety of reports indicated the potential for a widespread disruption of businesses by a virus.

The Case of Melissa

The creator of the Melissa virus combined a dash of deception to sweeten the poison. Melissa arrived in e-mails with the words, "Here is the document you asked for... don't show it to anyone else ;-) wink!" Attached was a document file which, when opened, dug into the user's address book and sent infected documents to the first 50 people on the list.

A computer epidemiological investigation began as systems around the globe fell ill. The investigators found that the file "passcodes 3-26-99," which would come to be known as the Melissa virus, was apparently first posted on the alt.sex newsgroup. Although the file appeared to be a list of passwords to porn sites, virus alarms went off owing to its real contents. The file was traced to a user with the e-mail address skyrocket@aol.com.

Meanwhile, a Swedish computer scientist tagged Melissa as the work of someone using the alias "VicodinES." Virus tools found on VicodinES's Web site had the name "Dave L. Smith" embedded in the source code. Further investigation determined that the skyrocket@aol.com account had been used by the virus writer to release the virus onto the Internet. The virus writer was traced by the FBI to a specific telephone in New Jersey. Less than a week after Melissa was released, Mr. Smith was arrested.

For a while, some computer experts pointed out that one positive result of the Melissa was that it raised users' awareness of the need for security measures on computers. However, subsequent events would show that memories are short when it comes to Internet security.

I LOVE YOU. VBS

Since the dawning of the new millennium, hundreds of malicious programs have been released on the Internet. Alerts warning of some new strain of electronic pathogen have been issued daily. New vulnerabilities are being reported at a rate of 40–80 per month "that is two new holes every day that can be exploited. There has been a corresponding increase in the number of exploits written to take advantage of these holes. Not surprisingly, given their market penetration and open architecture, most of these vulnerabilities and exploits are associated with the Windows and Linux products.

The "VBS.LoveLetter.A," a virus-Trojan-worm let loose in spring 2000, was characterized by industry leaders as "the most damaging and widespread outbreak ever," with at least "three times the 'byte'" of the Melissa virus, that itself had infected 1.2 million computers in North America and caused $80 million in damage. When the cost of VBS.LoveLetter.A. is finally tallied, it is likely to be in the billions.

The VBS.LoveLetter.A message carried a sinister payload as an attachment, and with the alluring subject heading "I LOVE YOU," propagated virulently as an e-mail or through Internet relay chat (IRC) channels. The attachment was written in the Visual Basic programming language and targeted machines running the latest version of Microsoft Internet Explorer/Outlook.

VBS.LoveLetter.A would execute if the recipient double-clicked (to open) the attachment, or in many cases, was executed by Windows automatically through the preview pane of MS Outlook. Once executed, VBS.LoveLetter.A would send an e-mail copy of itself to everyone in the victim's address book and onto IRC channels; overwrite a dozen types of files including music, video, and images; and download a Trojan horse program from the Web that in turn was designed to steal passwords and transmit them to an account in the Philippines.

The VBS.LoveLetter.A appears to have originated in the Philippines and struck Hong Kong early in the business day on May 4, 2000. Within two hours, it had infected computers worldwide in pandemic proportions. Days later, a dozen mutant strains and variants were discovered on the Internet.

The international investigation focused quickly on the Philippines. It was determined that the virus was initially released from two e-mail addresses, spyder@super.net.ph and mailme@super.net.ph, both of which belonged to the Manila-based Internet service provider Supernet. The owner of these addresses took steps to hide his identity by using a series of fraudulent and stolen e-mail addresses and anonymous, prepaid Internet-access cards. Nevertheless, 48 hours after the outbreak, the investigation had narrowed to a 23-year-old Filipino computer college student Onel A. de Guzman, and three others.

The computer college had earlier rejected Guzman's password-stealing-virus thesis, labeling it "illegal" and "unacceptable." Under retrospect examination, it appears the thesis closely resembled VBS.LoveLetter.A. Further investigation uncovered Guzman's membership in an underground computer club called GRAMMERSoft — a group well known to the local Internet service providers for hacking. The ISPs had complained on numerous occasions to Philippine authorities about GRAMMERSoft in the past.

The Virus Business

Inoculating computers against constantly muting virus strains is a $1.3-billion industry, rivaling real-world pharmaceutical companies. Today, most virus infections come though e-mail attachments and free software downloaded from the Net. The remaining infections are attributable to sharing diskettes. There have even been instances where anti-virus software was specifically targeted by viruses. Bitter irony was tasted by the infamous hacking group Cult of the Dead Cow when their tool Back Orifice 2000 (BO2K), handed out at the Defcon hacker conference, was found to be accidentally infected with the Chernobyl virus.

"It makes us look like idiots," they later commented.

Those professionals who track the evolution of computer viruses have noticed some unnerving trends:

» Just as viruses, Trojans, and worms are being combined, the many different exposures of a computer system are converging, where one vulnerability can be exploited many ways, and conversely the same exploit may work against many vulnerabilities.

» Computer networks are becoming more permissive as users demand more functionality. A system that computes and communicates at the speed of light is likely to pass viral infections at the same speed.

» As legitimate software applications benefit from increased interoperability, so will malicious code.

» The presence of e-mail and Web tunnels into corporate systems allow for mal-code and mal-ware to enter.

» The naïveté of users is exploited with simple deception by the malicious code writer.

Third-Party Liability

Transmitting viruses to customers or partners is not only anti-social and bad for business, but also can raise potentially costly liability issues. If someone's computer is hacked or attacked from your computer, to what extent are you liable? There is a great deal more discussion than litigation at this stage, with insurance companies, law firms, large corporations, and governments taking the matter seriously. We have begun to see the first few suits reach the courts. The prevailing thought is that if you have not taken reasonable steps to secure your computer system and it is subsequently compromised and used to attack another computer or a Web site, you could be sued for negligence.

The thorny point is determining what are reasonable precautions when it comes to computer security and the average person. It is reasonable to assume that a large corporation would be held to much more stringent security standards than the average person. As e-commerce grows and computer security issues become more widely known, so shall the expectations placed on individual users for protecting their systems and indirectly those of their neighbors.

The majority of cyber-attacks come from either Internet accounts obtained by fraudulent means or from compromised hosts belonging to innocent third parties. Usually, the third party does not realize that their computer has been broken in to and is being used to launch devastating attacks on other people. It is incumbent upon the third party to prove that they are not the ones originating the attack nor are they willing conspirators.

Establishing your innocence in such a matter can be troublesome if you have no security or electronic audit mechanisms in place to begin with. The lack of security safeguards could lead to charges of negligence; conversely, producing logs that vindicate you may expose you to criticism for not monitoring or acting sooner. This illustrates the need to establish a comprehensive security plan, with systems in place to ensure it is followed.

Devices

A sorcerer's magical devices include wands, hats, and orbs used to better channel his power. The necromancy of cyberspace has adopted tools for discovery, manufacturing access, and controlling machines. Here are just a few of the current favorites.

War Dialers

It is not uncommon for computers to have modems attached to regular phone lines, even if there is a network connection. Often, if someone rings the telephone number, a computer will answer. If it does, then access for an intruder is usually a matter of trying different accounts and passwords until one works.

The initial challenge for the threat agent is to find a telephone number with a modem and computer attached to the other end. A war dialer is a tool for just that purpose. It quickly and automatically dials a list or range of numbers, signals, then listens for a response by a modem. If successful, it notes the particulars of the exchange and moves on. Otherwise it just hangs up. In this way, lists of potential back doors can be assembled overnight.

These independent, remote modem connections bypass many network-security measures. It's like having a secret entrance to the castle.

Vulnerability Scanners

Vulnerability scanners are legitimate tools used by security professionals to quickly test computers and networks for common vulnerabilities. These scanners automate much of the laborious testing routine, allowing the professional to then concentrate on site-specific testing. Unfortunately, these tools are also available to anyone who wants to find vulnerabilities on a computer system, regardless of intent.

These vulnerability scanners (or assessment tools) test for a whole range of potential trouble spots, including permissions, weak passwords, trust relationships, known holes, access control, and susceptibility to denial of service attacks. They initially scan and probe the computer or network. Gradually, more provocative testing is performed, and the closer to the real thing it becomes. Testing for denial of service attacks often requires that you run the actual attack and see whether your computer falls over. If the system crashes, you know you are susceptible — it's like a doctor testing to see if you are allergic to gun shot wounds.

Eventually a report is generated. Recently hackers have gotten into the habit of posting the vulnerability profile of systems on the Internet for someone else to take advantage of.

Computer Microphones

Do you have a microphone or video camera installed or connected to your computer? If so, you may want to consider this: In a recent Minnesota legal case, an employee posted a picture of herself wearing shorts and a bathing-suit top on the company Web site. A manager was overheard by a coworker making some remarks about the photo, in the privacy of his office.

A harassment lawsuit was filed against the manager and surreptitious recordings made by the company from the manager's computer microphone were entered into evidence against the manager. The manager was fired, and the employee filed for $30 million in damages.

Are your conversations being monitored? Although illegal in most Western countries, the practice still goes on. Nearly every computer made after 1996 has a microphone. Software can pick up speech from a small office, compress and store it, or even send it over a local network or the Internet. Hackers can invoke this capability with tools like Back Orifice and pull the results back to themselves remotely — a fun way to invade your privacy, eavesdrop on confidential meetings about that great new product your company is about to launch, or record conversations that could be used for blackmail purposes.

Spells and Incantations

Much of the software used by threat agents is crudely packaged as "exploits" — simple programs that can have pathological effects. A skilled threat agent can string these exploits together to achieve the desired result. The most straightforward effect is to shut your computer down or cause it to crash. These are denial-of-service (DoS) attacks. Here are a few ways your computer can be upset:

IP Fragmentation

Information is sent to computers and received in "packets" — well-defined groups of ones and zeros. The computer needs to know precisely how long these packets are, in order to put them back together.

Fragmentation attacks work by setting the fragmentation offset to be inside the previous packet's payload (overlap or well outside). The system fails to reconstruct the packets and panics. The packets keep coming and the re-assembly work falls further behind until the system cannot recover. Exploits like this have amusing-sounding names like "Ipfrag teardrop," "newtear bonk," and "boink," but have less-than-humorous consequences.

Ping of Death

Large packets of data are not handled well by computers and may cause them to react apoplectically and crash. When this occurs, you will usually get a blue screen and a fatal error message. The computer has to be shut down by hitting the off switch, and recovering after a reboot (turning it back on).

A "ping" is normally a short "Hello" message sent between computers. The "ping of death" works by sending a very large packet whose payload is less than the maximum 65536 bytes, which allows it to exit the attacker's computer, but which expands once the headers (lines of text containing such things as addresses, error checking, and packet numbers) are added, exceeding the maximum a computer can handle, thus making the ping dangerous to the receiving computer — a hello from hell.

SYNflood

For computers to establish a dialog, they need to synchronize. There has to be some understanding as to who starts the discussion and then who listens and in what time sequence. A synchronization flood (SYNflood) attack attempts to overload a computer with a series of rapid synchronization requests. A synchronization request is the initial communication for establishing a connection with a computer, much like someone calling your name to get your attention — "Hey you, listen up!" — except in a SYNflood they keep calling over and over again. You cannot reply fast enough and eventually pass out with the effort. A fast network connection between the attacker and the victim is generally required to convey packets fast enough to confuse a computer in this way.

A specific version of this class of attack called "syn-hose" adds a twist by randomly "spoofing" the return address. The computer tries to answer hundreds of crank calls per second and blue screens. This is similar to walking in the woods and hearing your name called, "Hey you, answer me," in a different voice from behind every tree, and trying to react to each one.

Storm

A packet storm sends multiple packets to a port address on a computer that is reserved for broadcast. This same broadcast address is used as a "response to" or a "from" address on the message. The packets hit the computer's broadcast port and are sent to all other computers on the network segment. These ports all respond back to the broadcast port, which in turn re-broadcasts back to all the computers . . . and so on — traffic jam. The ensuing packet collision rates go critical.

A similar exploit called "Winack" sends a packet that appears to have originated from and is destined to the same address, thus causing a vicious circle of synchronization requests and acknowledgments requests. The targeted machine is left to scream at itself, like a dog chasing its tail.

Connection

A tool like the charmingly named "Port-Fuck" attempts to establish many communication sessions with the target computer, effectively wasting your machine's time and denying access to legitimate traffic.

Kill Session

A nasty exploit called "Sniper" kills a legitimate communications session your computer is having. In the real world, this is like someone briefly pulling your phone jack out of the wall when you are having a phone conversation.

DNS Spoofing

Rather than hacking into a communication channel to retrieve the information, it may be easier to reroute the communication to another site under the influence of the threat agent. This can be accomplished by either compromising routers (devices on the Internet that route traffic to destinations) between parties, or inserting fraudulent routing information to these devices.

Routers contain tables that map a domain name (www.company.com) with an Internet protocol address (e.g., 123.345.456.67). The tables also indicate the routes to get there. Domain name service (DNS) spoofing modifies these maps to re-route your communication somewhere else — like moving road signs around.

The result is that when you attempt to go to one site, you are instead brought to the fake site. In the case of Web sites, the forgery can be entirely convincing because any Web page can be easily copied in minutes. For example, on November 15, 1999, DNS spoofing occurred on Canadian government Web domains for an hour, perpetrated by the group atheists.Net.

Strategies and Tactics

It is the actions of the threat agent that bring these weapons to life and ultimately determine the severity of the outcome. Strategies and tactics in cyberspace parallel real-world military tactics, but to date are far less evolved. However, it is only a matter of time before cyber-weapons are used to their full potential.

Reconnaissance

Information-gathering activities targeting a network attempt to elicit details such as topology, addresses used, trust relationships, and connectivity. These actions amount to "doorknob rattling." The intent is reconnaissance in preparation for exploitation. The existence of reconnaissance activities changes the security posture of the system — it gradually becomes more exposed as the attacker learns more.

In information theory, a transfer of data is described as communication between a sender and receiver. In reality, data are passed in full "duplex" — both sender and receiver speak at the same time — with constant handshaking. The information is passed only in a virtual sense. Electrons or photons do not travel physically from sender to receiver; the telephone line only oscillates high and low voltage. This physical change is used to convey meaning, symbols, and ultimately information from the sender to the receiver. The conduit through which the communication occurs is referred to as the channel. While this communications channel appears to be the obvious place for a third party to tap in and intercept the communications, in reality this is a complex task. It is not as easy as depicted by Hollywood.

Interception

Although threats to information technology systems do not stem only from computers, the Netcentric threat is very real. Attacking computers with computers over networks is one of the most cost-effective ways of intercepting or acquiring sensitive information passing through or stored on those systems and ultimately transporting the data out of the target's computer.

These days, communications intercept has more to do with hacking computers than with scaling a telephone pole and physically tapping into the wires. Intercepting a communication between two parties can be extremely useful to a threat agent. Being able to influence the conversation or transaction in mid-stream can be profitable.

Manipulative deception attempts to impersonate a trusted entity (masquerading) or the information itself (spoofing). The "Man-in-the-Middle" attack is an implementation of a deception tactic where the threat agents place themselves directly within the communications path. It is a form of active intercept. Each of the parties in the legitimate conversation believe that they are speaking to the other directly, when in fact they are only speaking with the threat agent, who just relays the information back and forth. Because everything goes through the threat agent, he or she is privy to all the information and is also in a position to influence the conversation. A real-life example of this technique is the Zimmerman telegram, which was intercepted and modified by the British to successfully motivate the U.S. to become involved in the First World War.

Insertion and Replay

Insertion of foreign data into the communication path by the threat agent can occur during a man-in-the-middle attack or another active-intercept means of access. A variant of this is the "replay attack" which retransmits valid packets, reintroducing them into the communications. This would be similar to recording a "false alarm" transmission from the police-fire emergency radio band broadcasts, starting a fire, and then replaying the taped "false alarm" broadcast immediately after the call for the real fire was sent out.

Delay

Delaying the receipt of information is an effective attack tactic and a relatively easy one to deploy. Time-critical functions like trusted time stamp services, stock market transactions, and patent submissions are at risk from this type of attack. Imagine sending a message to your broker to sell, sell, sell a stock you know is going to fall, only to have your message deliberately delayed until after the stock's value has bottomed out.

Degradation

Degradation of communications signals can be an end in itself or a tool for making interception easier. Communications can be degraded by forcing them onto a secondary path that is slower or less secure. There have been cases of companies with good, secure network communications having their business deliberately transferred to a voice telephone line where it was intercepted by their closest competitor.

The Attack

The sophistication and nature of a cyber attack varies considerably, from the simple and indiscriminate (the equivalent of throwing rocks at moving cars) to the sophisticated, clandestine, and surgically targeted work of professionals (cyber-espionage).

Given the potions, devices and incantations, consider the following various forms of attack and keep in mind the expanding dimensions of cyber-sorcery and warfare. The deliberate attack involves the threat agent exploiting a system vulnerability in a decisive manner.

Surprise is the most effective element in executing a successful attack. Threat agents may use various combinations and permutations of attack tactics to achieve their aims. Here are just a few possible approaches:

» *Simple direct* — A threat agent acts with a single action against one vulnerability. The path of the attack is straightforward. Example: an older form of modem attack would send a series of letters and numbers in an e-mail that then mimicked a control command to the modem to shut it down. Whenever the victims tried to retrieve their e-mail, their modem would disconnect.

» *Simple indirect* — The attack is a solitary action but carried out from an oblique path. Example: a hacker launches a "ping of death" attack from a site they have previously compromised. The target may ask themselves, Why is this government department attacking me?

» *Progressive indirect* — Not only is the attack launched obliquely, but it is itself a composite of more than one attack, each capitalizing on the effects of the previous. The normal sequence is reconnaissance, access, exploitation, and denial. Example: network mapping followed by a Phf attack, password cracking, and so on.

» *Distributed coordinated* — An attack that is a composite of many attacks launched simultaneously from many different sources. Example: Java applet at a Web page which when loaded on all the visitor browsers launches an attack on a target site.

» *Attack by combination* — A progressive attack with a predetermined series of actions that have a history of being successful when launched in quick succession. Attacks of this type are usually automated. Example: an attacker may run two or more exploits against a system to "blue screen" the machine, where just one in isolation would not do the job.

» *Fragmented* — An attack that disguises its identity by splitting into parts small enough to go undetected. The time to reassemble and launch is usually less than the decision cycle of the target. The target reaction time is often compromised by lack of distance or by getting inside security parameters. Example: bypassing firewall proxies or intrusion detection systems by packet splitting.

» *Deception* — The target is faked into reacting in such a way as to reveal a vulnerability. Deception is usually required when the target has a good security posture. Example: masking — an attempt to cover or hide activities.

» *Tunneling* — Repackaging an attack within a legitimate transaction or code so as to bypass firewall rule sets or to hide malicious code. Example: Trojan horse program.

» *Immobilization* — Targeting the safeguards or attempting to slow reactive defenses, while acting against the exposed vulnerability. Example: Send a complex task to the intrusion detection system (IDS) to delay its response time; meanwhile, launch an attack on a network machine.

» *Timing* — Attacks can be based upon timing or respective decision cycles. Example: using the processing delay in the IDS to slip in a fast but effective DoS attack simultaneously from many spoofed IPs.

» *Attack on preparation* — This attack can be the most devastating because it is launched at the time when sites are most vulnerable. Example: a hit on the stock market computers as the market opens for the day or just before it officially closes.

» *Second intention* — An attack against a programmed counter to any attack. Example: an IDS will shun an IP that triggers an alarm based upon attack signatures (previous attack patterns). Given this knowledge, a threat agent will spoof the IP address using an address from a mission critical system instead. The IDS may in fact be tricked into blocking a legitimate function. DoS attacks can also be launched to solicit a response and thereby better acquire the true target.

» *Counter time* — Used against a good but predictable counter. A crude application of this tactic is to initiate constant interference with a communication channel to force it onto an alternate conduit where the threat agent may have better resources to attack the signal.

» *Broken rhythm* — A complex attack carried out with unpredictable timing — initial melee punctuated by lengthy apprehension, then decisive attack. One tactic is to draw the victim into attempting counter attack (or other desired reaction) and then attacking while they are just preparing to attack or react.

When discussing a cyber attack incident, military terms are often employed:

» *Engagement* — The exchange of defensive and offensive actions. Military forces in the future may find themselves in a cyber-engagement. At this time, actions/counter-actions resemble tit-for-tat skirmishes.

» *Decisively engaged* — This is the point when or where you cannot withdraw from an attack without suffering more of a loss; that is, the withdrawal would expose a critical vulnerability. Example: the defensive maneuver of shutting your system down to end an attack might do more harm than staying online to exorcise the attacker.

» *Disengagement* — Shifting away from the line of your initial attack, presumably because it was blocked, or to withdrawal. Hackers do this a lot — hit and run.

A system administrator also has some tools to use in war time:

» *Drawing* — Deliberately exposing a vulnerability to invite attack for the purposes of identifying attackers or riposting the attack. Takes advantage of the axiom that flagrant vulnerabilities invite attack. Example: the systems administrator creates a "honey pot" for hackers to play in. The hackers believe that they are breaking into a real system; meanwhile their activities are being monitored, controlled, and tracked.

» *Delaying action* — One can fight not to win but to delay losses or create a stalemate. This tactic is only useful as a prelude to disengagement or withdrawal, or when waiting for reinforcements like the police to arrive. A large telephone company may suffer phreakers long enough for the FBI to catch up with them. It is not profitable to shut the phone system down, nor do they want to lose the trace on the intruders completely.

Attack Impact

The nature of an attack is highly dependent upon the motivation and intent of the threat agent. Given the right tools, what happens to your computer is driven largely by the creativity and ingenuity of the threat agent, and may include activities related to search, survey, intercept, entry, acquisition, disclosure, manipulation, deception, modification or delay, implantation (covert channel), loss, theft, influence, propaganda, nuisance, suppression, neutralization, denial, disruption, destruction, intimidation — you get the idea! It is important to have a recovery plan in place; otherwise the impact of the attack can continue to resonate after the main incident — stolen passwords can be used; hidden code may be launched.

Cyber-Espionage

All the trade craft taught in spy school is found in its virtual form in cyberspace. The agents using them may work for governments or industrial competitors. They meet covertly in cyberspace or use an electronic dead letter box to drop information into and retrieve to avoid direct contact and association. The "brush meets" you see in old spy movies now happen in virtual space at the speed of light and are nearly impossible to catch. Unsuspecting sites are used as "cut-outs" to temporarily store information for later retrieval or as zombie machines to attack other computers. Secret agents communicate clandestinely from behind hostile territory using state-of-the-art steganography, cryptography, and the Internet.

Cryptography is the art of writing codes and ciphers. Cryptanalysis is the science concerned with violating, cracking, and compromising codes and ciphers. Both can be important tools for the high level spy. Many organizations safeguard their information by encrypting it, and being able to decipher that information is a significant talent. Cryptanalysis requires big talent and big bucks, so it's usually out of the range of most hackers. Big governments, big corporations and big criminal syndicates are the likely users of high-level cryptanalysis. Targets are usually other governments and corporations.

Conversely, encryption — encoding documents so that they can only be read by those who have the key to the code used — has become a relatively easy process. If you want to send more sensitive documents by e-mail, or are simply concerned with protecting your online privacy of individuals, encryption is worth looking into for your own documents. Small-time crooks look for targets of opportunity and the path of least resistance. Unencoded documents become targets merely because they're easy to read; for example, if you send your credit card number in an unencrypted e-mail that gets hijacked, it's easy picking. If that same e-mail has been encrypted and gets hijacked, decoding it is not worth the time and cost to the average credit card thief. It's a case of making yourself a less desirable target than your neighbor who doesn't take the same precautions as you.

Unless you are a spy yourself, you don't need to know much about deciphering. I discuss cryptography and cryptanalysis in greater detail in chapter 10, but here I will briefly cover one deciphering technique — the brute-force method — because it can be used by threat agents with little cryptanalytical knowledge. The brute-force method has been the one most often (publicly) used against modern crypto-systems. A brute-force attack is an exhaustive key search. The attacker tries every possible key in turn until the correct key to the code is found. To identify the correct key, it is necessary to monitor the text for recognizable characteristics or a match with known plaintext as you are attempting to decrypt it.

A popular use for the brute-force method is password cracking. Your password is usually encrypted and stored on your computer. A threat agent steals this file and tries every conceivable alphanumeric combination, starting with words found in dictionaries and common names. Weak passwords can be cracked through the brute-force method in minutes by the average hacker using automated tools such as L0phtCrack. These programs do not attempt to break the way your password was encrypted. Instead they take a string of characters, encrypt it the same way your computer did, and compare the result with your password file. If there is a match, then the string is your password. So if your password is Smith03, it will likely be cracked in minutes. Someone can steal this password by breaking in over the Internet or with a boot-up diskette and momentary physical access to your machine. An attack can also take advantage of configuration errors and poor or default passwords (like the word password) to gain unauthorized access to services. Most computer systems use a very simple encoding process known as "hashing," which is better used for message integrity checks than for protecting message confidentiality.

In reality, cryptanalysis attacks are the least cost-effective way of getting your information. An attacker will likely try another route when confronted with cryptography, or will give up on the attack altogether. Careful choice and protection of passwords as well as the use of an appropriate level of encryption can be a very good defense against intrusions on your privacy and theft of valuable data.

Chapter 7
Surfing with Sharks:
A Case Study

*H*ere I present a scenario to show how some of the schemes and devices I have described might actually be used. I have used a composite of real incidents that have occurred over the last 10 years to give this cautionary tale the ring of truth, but the names in this story are fictitious, and do not represent any real persons, groups or enterprises, living or dead. The software and techniques I describe are very real, however. You can be sure that history will repeat itself.

This is the story of LowTech Industries, a small company that planned to gain competitive advantage by embracing the Internet and e-commerce, and their subsequent loss of corporate innocence to the real dangers of the virtual world. It is also the story of how hackers insinuate themselves into a system before they strike.

Reconstructing events as they occurred in late 1999 . . .

The Good Guys

LowTech Industries was a promising company under the limited partnership of four siblings: a brilliant computer engineer, an award-winning videographer, a screenwriter, and a graphic artist. The company was established in 1998 and now employs a handful of computer graphics artists and technicians. At the time the events described below occurred, LowTech had become well known within the multimedia and entertainment business, producing corporate videos and DVDs, television commercials, and interactive multimedia (CD-ROMS and Web sites).

With their state-of-the-art digital video nonlinear editing suite, the LowTech post-production unit could create all those whiz-bang special effects and super realistic computer animation that you see at the movies. LowTech executives made a strategic decision to provide leading-edge Internet multimedia solutions to its corporate clients. Capabilities such as trend-setting Web site designs, QuickTime video streaming, and virtual reality walkthroughs paid off in gaining LowTech a sustainable competitive advantage in a hotly contested and volatile cyber-marketplace. LowTech Industries' corporate identity was showcased in their award-winning Web site, complete with the ability to offer secure e-commerce transactions, including online real-time credit card authentication and authorization using SSL and Web certificate technology.

Mindful of quality-of-life issues and in the interests of avoiding high property taxes, the partners had decided to locate LowTech Industries on the side of a mountain near Vancouver, British Columbia, Canada. The rooms in the chalet served as offices housing the computer graphics workstations and digital editing unit. Employees worked on high-end Silicon Graphics workstations or Apple PowerMacPC G4s with velocity engines capable of executing at least one billion floating-point operations per second or gigaflop (classified as supercomputers by the U.S. military). Each computer supported a hard disk array of at least 108 Gbytes or enough to store eight hours of full-motion digital video. (In comparison, this page is 0.000003 Gbytes in size.) Each workstation came with the new Apple 22-inch-wide cinema flat-screen display and surround sound system. All these computers were connected along a lightning-fast 100Mbps fiber optic local area network (LAN). You got the impression that there was a great deal invested in equipment there.

LowTech was housed in a characteristic and attractive chalet with a twist. You would notice that doors were protected with high-grade magneto-mechanical locks and an inconspicuous surveillance camera. This was part of a sophisticated access-control and alarm system consisting of passive infra red (PIR) motion detectors, contact switches on all the doors and windows, and electronic smart card readers for access into the server room. The system was monitored after hours by a local security firm. These measures were required by the insurance broker given the millions of dollars' worth of high-tech computer equipment.

If you were to walk in the front door of the LowTech headquarters you would find yourself in a common area equipped with a high-definition home theater. Some employees would be engaged in a free-flowing ideas session around the espresso machine, while others leaned back in high-backed comfortable chairs, creating at their laptops, which were in constant communication with the main server and each other by way of a high-speed wireless LAN. The smell of freshly baked bread would permeate the air.

The air-conditioned server room formed the hub of the operation, connecting everyone together and providing impressive online shared storage capabilities.

Gargantuan work projects could be passed between teams with remarkable ease.

LowTech was connected from its cozy and remote location to the outside world by way of a high-speed 20MBps microwave Internet connection to an Internet service provider (ISP) in town. Their telecommunication tools included regular telephones, voice mail, and faxes.

Typical electronic services such as Web browsing, e-mail, file transfers (FTP), Internet-phone, video conferencing, and directory name services (DNS) were required by all LowTech employees in the course of their work. In addition, the LowTech enterprise Web site was seen as providing an open channel of communications to the marketplace and clients, presenting a tangible image of the company. This channel had, in the last few years, become the critical marketing instrument for the company.

You can gain an appreciation for the level of investment and dependence on computers, electronic communication, and digital information assumed by LowTech. On Friday, March 26, 1999 (incidentally the birthday of one of the LowTech partners), the Melissa Macro Virus propagated through e-mail attachments over the Internet at large, causing widespread disruption to businesses, followed closely by the Chernobyl Virus in April and the ExplorerZip Trojan in June. These viruses damaged many Windows-based computers around the world. LowTech, being primarily a Macintosh-based enterprise, came through uninfected. However, the incidents and horror stories from the surrounding business community served to scare the company's system administrator (sys admin) into taking some precautions.

Virus scanning software was loaded onto all machines, which would quietly work in the background. All new files or programs were automatically scanned for viruses. The LowTech sys admin began to update the virus libraries once a month.

A firewall was installed at the communications gateway between the LowTech internal network and the external connection to the Internet service provider (open cyberspace). This firewall was set up to regulate the type of traffic permitted to enter or exit LowTech. The firewall itself consisted of a high-end Sun workstation running a version of the UNIX operating system and specialized firewall software. This firewall supported four logically separate connections or environments. One connection was the external route to the Internet (through the provider), the corporate Web server hung off another link, a server hosting both mail and FTP used the third, and the LowTech internal LAN used the last connection. The firewall was designed to manage the type and flow of information between these environments according to a set of rules that could be as strict or as lax as the sys admin allowed, in accordance with local security policy — if LowTech had one.

LowTech was a seriously wired enterprise seamlessly plugged into the Net. Its leading edge work in Web media technologies relied on innovation and freedom, ideals that provide a challenge to configuration management and security. With its resources devoted to sustaining competitive advantage, security was a secondary consideration. The sys admin was busy just keeping the complicated system up and running. The company management and he had agreed they needed to sit down sometime and do a thorough risk assessment, but there never seemed to be time. The firewall and virus scanner would probably do the trick anyway.

The Bad Guys

On August 6, 1999, three members of the GroundZero hacker group met at an Internet cafe in Chicago, Illinois,

U.S.A. They met there on the first Friday of every month in real life (IRL, as they say) to drink coffee and trade hacker knick-knacks in a more personal setting. Newer members had to endure almost a year of online vetting they were invited to meet established members IRL.

GroundZero had been formed five years previously by two college freshmen with a penchant for cyberspace skullduggery and arcane machine code. The two founders, who went by the aliases "Da3m0n" and "Gr3p," used the computers housed in the windowless basement of the university mathematics department to further both their academic and their extra-curricular vocations. The pair selectively talent scouted and recruited from the mathematics, science, and engineering departments. By graduation, GroundZero had grown to include ten disciples.

The motives of the group at this point were not so much sinister as they were exploratory and inquisitive. They took pride in their anonymity. Loose talk or unwarranted activities by any of its members brought quick discipline. Emphasis was placed on clandestine travel through interesting systems. Proficiency in UNIX programming and the ability to navigate through systems of that type were highly regarded skills. Members were encouraged to write their own exploits and try them out against other members of the group in a controlled fashion.

When Da3m0n and Gr3p graduated in 1998, the existence of the group had remained undiscovered by authorities. The founders left the university with more than just a degree; they also left with a keen knowledge of real world operating systems and networks. They were able to market these skills to a top software developer and were quickly assimilated into the high-tech work force in Silicon Valley.

The pair's Interest in GroundZero gave way to their new professions and new circle of friends. Da3m0n and Gr3p did continue to perform some low-key hacking activities, seeing it as professional development more than anything else. Occasionally, one of them would consult the active members of GroundZero about some particularly vexing problem, but for the most part their influence on the group's activities and motives was waning.

On that Friday night in the Chicago Cyber-Cafe, a new direction was debated amongst the group's lieutenants: "KaOs," "Sp1d3r," and "sybot." GroundZero had considerable talent within its ranks, and they were not content to remain in the shadows while there were over 30,000 hacker Web pages on the Net, many making outrageous claims. Word of GroundZero's elite skill set had been leaked to the underground by its members, no doubt with a measure of duplicity from the lieutenants. Many did not share the same level of enthusiasm the old guard had had for merely tinkering with the UNIX operating system. Given the allure of automated tool sets, the younger members were seduced by "the dark side."

As with the old guard, a keen understanding and sense of consequence had been naturally imparted to writers of unique hacking code in the course of development. But new, powerful software and virtual anonymity emboldened the group, eroding the notion of consequence from the simple act of a few mouse clicks. The player was now detached from the action. A decision was made to move GroundZero out from beneath its rock and into the ranks of the hacking elite.

First, the passwords to many more accounts and computer networks would be required to make a substantial impact. KaOs studiously pored over thousands of pages on her laptop while eating cheesecake and sipping a grande cappuccino. Each line represented the results of a vulnerability scan performed previously against an Internet protocol (IP) address using the latest vulnerability scanning tool, called "Nmap." This program was in vogue at the time owing to its ability to scan vast IP address spaces relatively quickly. The list in question included thousands of sites from around the world, and had been published on an electronic bulletin board (BBS) in Russia by German hackers. KaOs had resolved a great many of the numbers to domain names, which in turn represented real organizations. A few looked promising.

GroundZero consolidated their efforts over the next months to gather background information on potential targets. This information would be added to what was already available from each of their "black books" containing compromised sites — computers and accounts for which they already had passwords.

The early steps taken by GroundZero were that of passive reconnaissance, activities that were largely undetectable by the administrators of the targeted systems. Even so, all connections by the hackers to the Internet were made through accounts acquired under fictitious identities — throw-away, free Hotmail or Free-Net accounts, AOL accounts paid for with cash, or better yet, abandoned university accounts of students no longer with the university. Publicly available Internet services were used in their research methods, which included querying commercial search engines, using "reverse nslookup" to resolve IP addresses to a domain name (www.lowtech.com), and searching the "whois" databases that detail registration information for those domains. One can go straight to the corporate site by simply cutting and pasting either the IP or domain address into the URL line of a Web browser, then just hit return and read with a malicious eye.

This is how the GroundZero hackers gathered much preliminary information on their targeted corporate entities and attempted to gain visibility into their computers and networks. The exercise allowed the group to focus their efforts on those targets that were either especially vulnerable or especially lucrative. LowTech was one of the sites to make the short list.

Over the remaining summer period, two dozen sites were compromised by GroundZero. Back doors were established on target systems. Key information was tucked away in black books, and sys admins were none the wiser — for the moment.

In the autumn of 1999, GroundZero turned its attention to LowTech. This corporate target was attractive to the hackers due to its potential processing capabilities and high-speed Internet connections. These system qualities are desirable because they permit automated hacking sequences such as flooding-type denial of service (DoS) attacks to be launched with relative ease and with a greater probability of success. The large storage capacities advertised on the LowTech corporate Web site would come in handy for stockpiling "warez" (pirated software).

Initial World Wide Web and newsgroup searches provided enough material to make some educated guesses about the LowTech system configuration, what services were provided online, and the nature of the information that lay within.

The next step was to investigate LowTech's system more directly, but here the hacker team would have to be very cautious. Approaching the target with heavy probing would raise the suspicions of an alert administrator. So, without knowing more about the security defenses of LowTech, light reconnaissance using techniques that closely mimicked typical computer network traffic would be the most prudent path.

Thus began the process of stealth scanning using techniques that are overlooked by most intrusion detection systems, firewall alarm logs, and other security mechanisms. The hackers distributed the workload; each would probe a set of the address space and port numbers from a different location over the Internet. These very slow and dispersed network scans would make historical analysis unfeasible. Each Internet address can have 65,000 ports with potential services associated with them. Think of it as your house having a civic address and 65,000 possible entry points. The trick is for the intruder to rattle the door handles and window latches without being detected.

The actual probing was accomplished using inverse mapping, in which innocuous acknowledgment packets are sent to a port. Where hosts do not exist, a "host unreachable" message will be returned. Active ports and services return a response indicating the ports are alive. Because no official connection is made, these probes are rarely logged. The analogy is calling the targeted house on the telephone, hearing the answering machine, and hanging up immediately. We could confirm that someone is actually living there, but no message is left and there is no flashing red light to show the occupant that a call attempt occurred. By determining which hosts exist and what ports and services are active, the hacker can gain valuable intelligence about the structure of the target's network.

At this juncture the GroundZero hackers had confirmed that LowTech was connected to the Internet though a single gateway at a provider named Wavetrek Inc. LowTech was allocated a block of IP addresses or "sub-net" off of a larger Class C network belonging to the provider. This would be important information because the hackers eventually wanted to narrow the target space. Further steps would be detectable by an alert system administrator, but would be necessary to make headway. In any case, the actions could be kept unintrusive and non-provocative so as to escape notice.

A tool called "discovery" was used to confirm the network's topology, and an attractive, three-dimensional graphical representation of it was automatically rendered after only a few minutes. The result displayed connectivity through the ISP to LowTech, and identified software versions, machine names, and trust relationships. Knowing which computers intrinsically trust each other is important for masquerading. More probing utilities in GroundZero's toolboxes were turned onto the address space. Programs like the graphical network scanner "Cheops," or more traditional ones like "tcpscan," and "fping," gave much the same results. The ISP's finger gateway was also used to search for LowTech identities. All in a night's work.

The material was shared at a hasty interim meeting of GroundZero at someone's dorm. The probe results had looked good on the surface, but some of the more experienced of the group saw potential problems. The results of the initial scans had indicated that all 64,000 ports on all of LowTech's IP addresses supported active services, where maybe a dozen at most would have been expected. Furthermore, there was only one LowTech machine present. Upon closer examination the group realized that this machine was aptly named "fw_gargoyle" — the first line of defense. The LowTech firewall was designed to respond to all probing on any port with a positive acknowledgment as a deliberate security measure to deceive broadband port scans. Everything behind the firewall was hidden to the hackers, and they still did not know what ports were really open. The original vulnerability scan from the list was also called into question.

One of the more industrious GroundZero crew members had written a Perl script for the "Netcat" tool that could be used to perform a more complete connection to each port. Over the next few nights and during mornings when he did not have any classes, Mr. Sp1d3r monitored the tens of thousands of connection attempts. Truly active ports would fully connect and wait for either legitimate traffic or for a command to disconnect, whereas inactive ports were dropped automatically. The payoff was that all of the expected services were in fact present. LowTech had Web access, e-mail, ftp, and a few others. And then there was one or two non-standard high ports open. Curious — maybe they were for remote access or special applications?

GroundZero had been able to crack every Web server they came up against like a hot knife through butter, except for the space agency, whose Web site was defaced by another hacker before they could finish. But the Web server at LowTech had confounded them. After nearly a week of nightly work, neither the Web, the e-mail, nor the file server yielded. And it was not for want of trying. Every intrusive exploit they could think of was attempted short of denial of service attacks, which would have given the game away. But none of their accounts originating the scans was ever counter-scanned, pinged, or queried either. So at least the hackers could assume that logs at LowTech were not monitored or analyzed.

And in this assumption, the GroundZero group was correct. LowTech had been very prudent in establishing their network from the beginning. They had hired a network security firm to install and configure the firewall and publicly accessed servers less than a year ago. So long as things did not fail badly, all was well, and the LowTech system administrator had more pressing matters to attend to than sifting through firewall logs.

GroundZero needed some time to regroup, and for a time LowTech was given a reprieve. The hackers instead focused on targets of opportunity — easy prey — and their black books filled with sites that GroundZero could own. Nevertheless, the LowTech file remained a thorny issue, if not somewhat of a personal embarrassment to some of group, most notably Sp1d3r, who felt that a bit of retribution against the recalcitrant target was in order.

The Hack

With tenacity and ingenuity, one can accomplish much. Sp1d3r had both, and was practiced in deception. He had been prowling about Wavetrek, LowTech's ISP, using the automated network vulnerability scanners "KANE," "NESSUS," and "SAINT."

The SAINT scanner is ironically the spawn of the Security Administrator Tool for Analyzing Networks (or SATAN) and has perhaps found more use within the hacking community than with system administrators.

SAINT (the Security Administrator's Integrated Network Tool) is freely available and has seen widespread use throughout the Internet community. In its simplest mode, SAINT gathers as much information about remote hosts and networks as possible by examining the presence of various network information services as well as potential security flaws — usually in the form of incorrectly set-up or configured network services, or of well-known bugs in system or network utilities. It can then either report or act upon the findings. A great deal of general network information can be gained using this tool: network topology, network services running, and types of hardware and software being used on the network. The results are displayed to the user in an easy-to-read Web page format.

The real power of SAINT is in its exploratory mode. Based on the initial data collection and a user-configurable rule set, it will examine the avenues of trust and dependency on a network. Not only is it generally considered to be anti-social to scan someone else's hosts or networks without the explicit permission of the owner, it is illegal as well. The dangers of SAINT stem from system crackers, potential intruders, indiscriminate use, or vulnerability scans that run beyond their borders. Many of the probes used by SAINT parallel the attack methods of criminal hackers (or "crackers"). The dangers of writing SAINT are tangible as well. According to the SAINT creators" Web site, one of its authors lost his job because of it, and there has been a letter-writing campaign to stop the release of the program. People have accused the creators of writing it for publicity and pure personal gain.

SAINT and the other tools allowed Sp1d3r to test the ISP's network computers at a rate beyond what would be humanly possible using manual methods. A SAINT heavy scan detected standard Windows NT NetBIOS ports open. The NetBIOS Auditing Tool (NAT) was run against the NT machines on the provider's network. NAT is an utility that goes after names and machine passwords. Although the default passwords had been changed, the encrypted password files were revealed by the NT and retrieved by the bad guy. Sp1d3r took these files and ran a brute-force cryptanalysis software utility called "L0phtCrack" against it. L0phtCrack, released by L0pht Heavy Industries (an elite hacker group), works by methodically searching through a dictionary of words and random characters, encrypting each word string using the same method ("hashing"), looking for matches. The operation was distributed over numerous computers at Sp1d3r's disposal and left running overnight. By morning, there were five password matches, and he was in.

Sp1d3r found that he was not alone. "Rootkit" had been installed on at least one of the network machines and there was other evidence that the provider had been entirely compromised by another hacker group. It looked as if the group had in fact closed off several security holes in the provider's network to consolidate their exclusivity.

Capitalizing on the other group's hard work, including saved password files, Sp1d3r gained greater access and used Rootkit to cover his tracks. He seized the opportunity to install his own sniffer called "Ethereal" to monitor all traffic between LowTech and the Internet.

A sniffer is like tapping a phone line; it works by placing the Ethernet (network) card of a given computer in promiscuous mode so that the hacker can "listen" to all traffic on that network segment. Normally the network card only pays attention to information addressed to that specific machine. The sniffer typically eavesdrops and sends the intercepted traffic back to its owner, but another neat trick it does is allow the hacker to insert data on the network segment if so inclined.

Next, Sp1d3r isolated the root passwords to the domain name servers (DNS) and was in a position to change things around a bit later. He would convince GroundZero to let him freelance on this one. The group had planned to act in a consolidated campaign of Web defacement and other tricks at 12 midnight, on the Eve of Hallows, October 31, 1999.

The sniffer output was substantial, and eventually Sp1d3r had to enlist the help of KaOs to sort through it all. Much of sniffer output generally needs to be interpreted — categorized in terms of types of traffic or patterns. Much of it is ones and zeroes, with the occasional clear ASCII text string. Both e-mail and Web traffic is easily readable. Sp1d3r and KaOs gained visibility into the inner workings of LowTech from this source. Now it was possible to construct a list of employees in LowTech and gain a rough appreciation of their duties. They isolated the system administrator's e-mail to help@lowtech.com and sysadmin@lowtech.com in short order. They could see that he subscribed to a variety of information technology (IT) mailing lists and bulletins.

The next night, armed with this information and highly caffeinated, the pair prepared the devices with which their technical prestidigitation would be played out. KaOs was able to connect from the Internet to TCP port number 25 (the default e-mail port) of a software firm — 3Wsoft Inc. It was the same company, incidentally, that provided the Web server software used by LowTech (a tidbit the hackers had discovered early on during reconnaissance of the LowTech site). From there, KaOs emulated a mail program and sent an e-mail message to sysadmin@lowtech.com. The e-mail message was transferred properly by the server at 3Wsoft Inc. By this means, the unwitting firm was used to relay a forged e-mail message. It appeared at LowTech Industries to have originated from their Web server software provider 3Wsoft Inc., and read:

```
From:    root@3Wsoft.com
Sent:    October 5, 1999 2:47 PM
To:      sysadmin@lowtech.com
Cc:      info@cert.org
Subject: URGENT SECURITY ADVISORY
```

It has come to our attention that the version of software you are currently running for your Web server is susceptible to a buffer overflow condition. It is advised that you download the most recent patch for this condition from our Web site www.3Wsoft.com/patches/buf_003.exe

Sincerely,

3Wsoft Inc., Web Security Representative

The masquerade was nearly complete. While KaOs was bouncing fictitious e-mails off servers, Sp1d3r had constructed a duplicate or "mirror" of the real 3Wsoft Web site complete with directories down to the finest details, with a minor change. The buf_003.exe patch was modified to include a Trojan program called NetBus (more about this later). Note that the software company's real Web site was not compromised, but rather a copy was made. This mirror site was actually stored on a local account right at WaveTrek.Net (the provider). The translation tables on the domain name server at this provider had been altered so that when someone like LowTech tried to go to the 3Wsoft site they were instead diverted to the mirror site under GroundZero's control. This was like switching street signs to lure tourists into the seedy part of town.

The bait was laid and all that was required was to drive the prey towards the trap. It was Sp1d3r who came up with the idea of launching a denial of service attack against the firewall, effectively taking down LowTech services, in hopes that this would spook the sys admin into downloading the Trojaned code from the fake Web site. During the next evening in Chicago or the business day in Vancouver, a SYNflood attack was launched on the LowTech firewall from one of GroundZero's previously compromised sites. It was an attempt to crash the targeted machine by overloading it with synchronization requests (the initial communication for establishing a connection). These types of assaults typically need fast network connections to be successful — a connectivity that LowTech had. The specific flavor of SYNflood used was an exploit called "Synhose," which launched a barrage of syn requests, each one from a randomly spoofed Internet address — much like a thousand people calling your name at once. The attack overloaded the buffers of the firewall nearly instantaneously and the machine was forced to abruptly reboot. It all happened so fast that nothing was logged. For a few minutes LowTech was blind to the outside world.

This process was continued throughout the day at regular intervals, and it was not long before people inside and outside of the company were complaining. The administrator was at a loss for an explanation. Then came another e-mail, this time from root@wavetrek.net (their

Internet service provider), forwarding the original 3Wsoft security advisory. The new e-mail indicated that customers had experienced attempts against their Web servers and urged them, as 3Wsoft had, to install the patch. This e-mail was addressed to not only the sys admin but the LowTech principals as well. This had been KaOs's idea — you see, this latest e-mail had been spoofed as well.

Manufacturing Access

To the delight of Sp1d3r and KaOs, the LowTech system administrator, finding himself between a rock and a hard place, visited the mirror site, downloaded the Trojaned patch from the Web server console, then double clicked on the patch buf_003.exe icon to execute it. Now this was a real patch for the Web server, and it did what the programmers had intended, but in the background, "NetBus" was activated.

Officially, the NetBus program is marketed as a remote administration tool, but it is nearly identical to the product named "Back Orifice," released by the Cult of Dead the Cow hacker group. Both of these programs are distributed freely on the Internet and have become all the rage for hackers. Both the Computer Emergency Response Team Coordination Center (CERT/CC) in the U.S. and the CANCERT in Canada have reported widespread use of NetBus and Back Orifice since their release. Professional tools of this ilk normally require registration and control mechanisms that tie the program's use to only a registered user. Neither NetBus nor Back Orifice has this functionality. The de facto purpose of NetBus is to acquire information, to intercept data traffic, and to control a targeted computer over the Internet. NetBus consists of a server-part and a client-part. The server-part is a program that exists on the target computer, while the client-part provides a GUI control for the attacker.

NetBus by default operates on TCP port 12345, but can nominally be reconfigured to use any port. Sp1d3r and Ka0s had chosen a high-numbered port typically used for ephemeral outgoing Web traffic that would most likely go unnoticed. The firewall rules would permit the connection of the Web browser to the outside world.

The Trojan installed itself in the background and provided Sp1d3r and Ka0s with astonishing control over the LowTech Web server, allowing them to

- » open/close the CD-ROM;
- » show an optional image on target screen;
- » swap mouse buttons — the right mouse button gets the left mouse button's functions and vice versa;
- » start any application;
- » play a sound file;
- » point the mouse to optional coordinates using their own mouse;
- » show a message dialog on the screen, with the answer always sent back to the hacker;
- » send the target Web browser to any URL;
- » send keystrokes to the active application on the target computer unseen;
- » capture any or all keystrokes and send them back to themselves;
- » take a screen dump and see what the target sees;
- » retrieve information about the target computer;
- » upload or download, delete, copy, or move any file from their own computer to the target computer;
- » increase and decrease the sound volume;
- » record sounds the computer's microphone catches — listen to everything said in the room;

» tap the computer's Web cam and see what was going on in the server room;
» disable any keys on the keyboard;
» show, kill, and focus windows on the system; and
» shut down or reboot the system.

The hackers communicated to the Trojan program remotely over the Internet by way of a virtual encrypted channel. The firewall would log all this traffic as a normal Web browsing session. The program (NetBus) remained hidden in memory. Virus scanners failed to detect it because it had been classed as a legitimate commercial utility and not malicious code by the virus protection vendors.

The next time the LowTech system administrator logged into the Web server, his key strokes were captured by NetBus and sent to an electronic dead letter box (a place where one can deposit messages to be retrieved by another party so that no direct connection is made) established in a foreign country and controlled by GroundZero. At two o'clock in the morning, the box was serviced by a remote automated script through an "anonymizer" in Norway that stripped off all address information and re-sent it using a different source address. The passwords ultimately ended up in the hands of KaOs.

The first thing she tried was to use this Web server password to remotely log into the firewall over that mystery high port 6,000 that the group had discovered earlier. Guess what — it worked. The administrator had reused his password on more than one machine. He was a busy man and occasionally had to log in from home to do his job. Remote access was a lot more convenient than driving up the mountain, he had too many passwords to remember, and he took what he thought was a calculated risk. Now the hackers had likely gained root access, meaning an account with super user privileges and ultimate control over the LowTech network.

Sp1d3r and Ka0s spent the remainder of that evening establishing additional secret accounts with super user and administrator privileges, modifying audit logs, securing any holes they found, and otherwise cleaning up their tracks and consolidating their position. They opened and secured a conduit through the firewall to the internal corporate network in Vancouver as they sat in Chicago. The consequences for LowTech now were limited only by the creativity and tenacity of GroundZero.

Meanwhile, LowTech Industries artists were busy working on their biggest project to date. A major motion picture studio had commissioned LowTech to create the trailer for the upcoming Christmas release of *CyberThreat — The Movie*. Over two hundred million dollars had gone into the production of the feature and it was forecasted to do well at the box office. Marketing was crucial to attracting the numbers envisioned. The trailer was to play in theaters starting in November 1999, but prior to that LowTech was contracted to establish a Web site complete with Web streaming Quick Time video previews and a virtual reality walk-through. A year earlier, the film *The Blair Witch Project* had been made for under $40,000 and had gone on to gross $120 million. Much of that film's success had been attributed to its aggressive online marketing campaign. This phenomenon was not lost on the major movie studios.

CyberThreat — The Movie was in the same genre as films like *Sneakers* and more recently *Hackers,* both of which had become part of hacker pop culture. This made the newest movie *CyberThreat* an ideal candidate for pre-release Internet promotion, and LowTech was simply the best company to pull it off.

Sp1d3r and Ka0s surfed, browsed, and rummaged through the LowTech corporate network like kids in a candy store, and it was not long before they came across the *CyberThreat* movie project files — 50 Gbytes" worth. There were Web design folders containing html (hypertext markup language) files used in building and displaying Web pages — perhaps they could make some design changes themselves before the page even went online. And then it struck them: The hard disk drives contained not only the movie's as-yet unreleased trailer but also the digital rendering of the entire film! LowTech Industries had been given an advance copy of the movie by the studio so that they could use it to construct the online promotional trailer. The copy was under strict conditions of non-disclosure.

CyberThreat — The Movie had been eagerly awaited by the hacker/cracker/phreaker community. Now Sp1d3r and Ka0s had it for themselves! This was the major coup they had envisioned, and it couldn't wait until the next scheduled meeting of GroundZero at the downtown coffeehouse. Calls were made before classes the next day. The traditional means of communication for GroundZero relied upon a meeting online, by logging into an Internet relay chat (IRC) session at a prescribed time and establishing a private chat room. Even with encryption, this was risky. Best they meet in real life (IRL) at a safe house this time.

Sp1d3r and Ka0s chortled as they explained their plans to the group. The action would set them and GroundZero within the ranks of elite hackerdom overnight. A few challenges remained, however. How does one download a multi-Gigabyte file without drawing attention, and what does one do with it?

In the end, they decided to click and drag the key movie files to the industrial digital video disk (DVD-RAM) write drive on LowTech's network. A DVD-RAM disk was mastered. The drive door slid open automatically melodramatically after the procedure. Sp1d3r authored a system message to the workstation hosting the DVD-RAM burner stating: "Warning! — Disk flawed — Dispose." The plan was to coax an employee to now throw the disk away. One of the members of GroundZero had a contact in Vancouver who had agreed to Dumpster-dive for what he was told was a CD-ROM.

But for whatever reason — maybe the disk was never disposed of, or the contact never panned out or could not get transportation to LowTech's remote location — the disk never came in the mail. So Contingency Plan B was set in motion.

GroundZero turned to a government server, pirated in days past and held in reserve, to act as the receiving host. It met the ideal specifications of high-speed connectivity, massive storage capacity, and location far away from Chicago. Ka0s used a cloned international cell phone hooked into her laptop to dial a long distance number into a large American provider's point of presence in Sweden. Then, through a series of anonymous accounts, the commands were given to copy the files from LowTech to the government site over a covert virtual channel.

Ironically, some of the best Web page designs are those of hacked pages. I guess it is the care and pride that goes into the work. GroundZero had fun coming up with the artwork for over three dozen sites they planned to attack, including that of LowTech. Each hacked design was tailored to mock the site's actual organization and baited their owners with a really cool GroundZero animated logo and background sound, plus the theatrical trailer to *CyberThreat,* framed with the credit "Starring GroundZero."

So, at midnight on Halloween 1999, the front page (index.html) of each site was hacked. Simultaneously, an anonymous (untraceable) message was posted to the alt.2600 hacker Web site and a slew of newsgroups giving the password to the government site where a full version of the movie was stored. A copy of the GroundZero news release, claiming responsibility for the hacks, was sent to dominant hacker Web sites and commercial news networks. Then the GroundZero hacking club went trick-or-treating.

The Sad Ending

When the GroundZero hack came to light, the principals of LowTech Industries were aghast. But the worst was still to come. News of the crack made the front pages of newspapers across the continent. The irony of a movie about hackers being itself hacked was not lost on the media and tabloids. A counterfeit version of *CyberThreat — The Movie* surfaced in Asia. The film studio sued LowTech for breach of trust and negligence for failing to provide adequate security safeguards given the original $250 million production costs for the movie. LowTech Industries was forced into bankruptcy. The hackers were never caught.

The Happy Ending

When the GroundZero hack came to light, the principals of LowTech Industries were alarmed. But in a brilliant marketing ploy, news of the incident was spun into an impromptu marketing campaign for the movie, thereby managing to squeeze victory from the jaws of defeat. The irony of the hack generated extraordinary publicity for the film both on- and off-line. The exact method of the hack was reconstructed into a spiffy TV promotion. The issue was raised in the public consciousness. By the time *CyberThreat — The Movie* screened at Christmas, it had pre-sold enough tickets to turn a hefty profit.

Safeguards

Even if the Happy Ending came to pass, LowTech Industries would have learned a few lessons from their hacker experience. Chastened but wiser, the company would set out to upgrade their security systems. So here's the coda to the Happy Ending:

A recent graduate from an information systems security program was hired as the assistant system administrator. His primary portfolio was that of security. Anthony went to work immediately. Remote access to the firewall was shut down, and the overall rule set governing information flow to and from LowTech was tightened up. All sensitive files and communications were encrypted using the Entrust Enterprise–level encryption products. The passwords were changed on all machines using names with eight random characters. Hardware devices called tokens were put into use on sensitive systems for two-factor authentication. The system was swept for and cleansed of Trojans. A protective watermark was digitally added to all of LowTech's digital videos, which would prevent unauthorized copying and digitally stamp the videos with the appropriate trademarks. The packet filtering routers at the Internet service provider were programmed to block unwanted data coming to LowTech. Personal desktop firewalls were installed on every machine to act as final gateways into each computer, allowing only authorized programs on the computer to communicate over select ports.

In much the same fashion as the door and motion alarms were installed at the building and monitored by an external security firm, LowTech hired a government-approved information technology security (ITS) firm to install and monitor a network intrusion detection system (IDS). The IDS was placed in front of the firewall, stopped and alarmed for known network attacks. The logs were reviewed and analyzed by the IT security firm and the reports were sent to the LowTech security officer, who compared them with firewall and system logs.

POSTSCRIPT

Ironically, shortly after I wrote this semi-fictitious story, the cryptographic copyright protection mechanism for digital video disks was compromised, delaying the sale of DVD music players a year. In other recent news, a new movie was stolen and posted on the Internet prior to its release at theaters. The investment in a major motion picture is enormous. Yet the end product can be contained in a 2.5GByte file on a DVD. The speed and power of home computers and the evolving communications capacity of the Internet make it feasible to copy the data stored on a DVD and distribute it illegally over the Net. The length of feature films has precluded widespread illegal copying and distributing over the Internet thus far. However, music is much easier to steal. The manufacturers and distributors of music DVDs needed strong copy protection and electronic watermarking of their products to prevent illegal copying. They thought they had it until the software to crack the copy protection was posted on the Internet a week after the protection scheme became known.

Chapter 8
Effective Risk Management

By now you should have a better understanding of the dangers lurking in cyberspace. Indeed, you may have decided to forego the Internet altogether. But let me remind you that, for all this discussion of mischievous hackers and potential cyber-terrorists, the Internet and its users are for the most part engaged in positive and constructive activities.

In any case, it is becoming more and more difficult to avoid using the Internet. I recently bought a new computer and, for the first time, I did the shopping and buying online. Not because I wanted to, but because I *had* to. I could not find a retailer in the country who stocked the new computer or the graphics software I wanted. It appears to be a trend in industries like music distribution, book-selling, and high-tech to sell directly over the Internet and avoid retail outlets altogether — check out the Apple Store or Dell On-line or Amazon.com.

However, as a consumer, I prefer to see the item in the store, touch and feel it, know that it is real. I am still leery about purchasing big-ticket items over the Internet. Even though Internet transactions account for only about two per cent of total business, according to VISA

International half of all credit card disputes involve repudiation of Internet transactions. VISA found that only five per cent of consumers trust online credit card transactions. Giving my VISA over the phone or across the Internet is still not as comfortable as making the transaction in person, even though the store itself uses the Internet to transmit the purchase information to the credit card company or the bank.

In the future, you will go to the store for some products and order online for others. It will become increasingly difficult to avoid using the Internet either as a consumer or businessperson. According to a managing partner at Anderson, "E-commerce is not only changing the way business is conducted; it is changing the fundamental economic assumptions on which business is based." A denial of service attack for Internet-based companies can mean immediate loss of revenue flow. Take for example the online auction house eBay: Hackers precipitated an outage in the summer of 1999 that cost the company an estimated $2 million in lost business.

Avoiding the Internet is not the way to deal with the various cyber threats I have described. On the other hand, continuing to use the Net for personal and business purposes without implementing some level of security is foolhardy. Assessing the risk of an attack on your home and business computer systems and developing a cost-effective plan to manage that risk will allow you to continue to enjoy the wonderful things the Internet offers. In fact, it may even enhance it. Polls show that most consumers are concerned about intrusions on their privacy and question the security of online purchases. With greater assurance of privacy and protection against fraud, you and your customers may feel more confident about using the Net.

You will recall the concept of risk assessment discussed in chapter 1. If you've read through the book this far then you should be better prepared now to make an assessment of your assets and vulnerabilities. In chapters 9 and 10 we will explore ways of protecting yourself, but first, knowing precisely what it is you need to protect will help you choose the safeguards to employ in your home and your business.

We are living in an age where wealth is ever more closely associated with information, and where technology has become both an enabler and a source of liability. Understanding your information assets is sometimes more elusive than some physical thing that you can hold and touch. To help us appreciate the value of information, the practice of the security community has been to identify inherent properties of information that need protection. What are the properties of your information systems that you would protect?

» *Confidentiality* — Information that is private or sensitive should not be disclosed to unauthorized individuals, entities or even some computer software processes. Some examples of things that you would want to keep confidential are trade secrets, product developments, business plans, private financial statements, health records, and salaries.

» *Integrity* — Data you do not want to have altered or destroyed in an unauthorized or accidental manner. Financial transactions are a key example of something you want unalterable.

» *Availability* — Can you get access and use the information, service, or communications channel when you need it? You need your telephone and Internet connection to be up. If you are a stockbroker, for example, market information must be available to you in near–real time.

» *Authenticity* — Is this the right information, service, Web site or person? When you file your tax form electronically, you need to be sure that it really is the tax department you are sending it to.

» *Accountability* — Ensures that the actions of an entity can be traced uniquely. If you conduct online banking, both you and the bank must be held responsible for the deposits and withdrawals.

» *Reliability* — The system must operate consistently and correctly; and

» *Non-Repudiation* — The ability to limit parties from refuting that a legitimate transaction took place. If a dispute arose, how would you prove that you did or did not make that online credit card transaction?

Few people would dispute that information and its supporting technology should be safeguarded. Where opinions vary is the extent to which security measures should be taken. Just how much hacker insurance do you take out? The determination of what is an acceptable risk depends upon the value of what you are trying to protect, the perceived likelihood of a threat event occurring, and the consequences of a successful attack.

As a computer user connected to the Internet at home and in your business, you need to weigh the consequences of not going online with the potential impact and likelihood of an attack. Risk management is not about eliminating risk entirely, but living with it. Firstly, the computer user must attempt to understand the threats and vulnerabilities. Only then can the user take steps to mitigate the exposures. There will always be some residual risk regardless of how much money is thrown at the problem, and a degree of uncertainty tied to any assessment of risk. You will have to decide if your assets are worth the effort. Self-defense is not enough. History has taught us that a purely defensive or passive posture will not withstand a persistent attack. A pro-active approach is recommended. In some cases this may simply mean holding back an attack long enough to have the service provider or police take the attacker off-line.

Poachers and Gatekeepers

In the world of information operations or security intelligence there are gatekeepers and there are poachers. If you are considering your own computer security, it is useful to approach the problem from both perspectives.

The gatekeeper implements established and best security practices regardless of the threat: if there are gaps, you plug them; if a door is open, you close it. Start by doing the easiest things first, whether they be installing the latest security patches or modifying your surfing practices. There is a good chance you will protect your interests adequately by doing a few simple things that have been shown to improve security posture in the majority of cases.

Practicing security through obscurity, or hiding your assets, is not a good approach. The poacher will take the path of least resistance. By placing yourself into this mindset you can adjust the placement of safeguards and detection devices. Note the threat environment is dynamic and that for every action there is a reaction. Hardening the front door may entice the thief to come in through the window. Thus, security measures should be implemented uniformly and with human nature in mind.

What is Your Risk?

Ask yourself who the threat agents are (hackers, fraudsters, commercial competitors, organized crime), and what is it you have that would interest them (proprietary information, high-speed Internet access, an identity, electronic cash, a launch site). Draw a line logically in your mind connecting the threat agents and your computer. The likely path they would take is dependent upon the means at their disposal, motive, intentions, potential benefit, opportunity, and the affordability of mounting the attack.

You provide the opportunity by revealing vulnerabilities in the setup of your system and in your computing practices. Just as in the wild outdoors, in the wild Web vulnerability invites attack from the predator. Learn not to behave like prey.

Chapter 9
Practicing Safe Surfing

*I*nformation is a valuable commodity, and today the easiest way to compromise information is by computer through electronic connections. Thankfully, there are some simple and inexpensive things you can do to mitigate the risks. Real information security involves people, processes, and technology. In this chapter we will focus on people and processes. Most of the suggestions here involve using your brain and the options already available in the software you're using to access the Internet. In chapter 10 we'll look at the more technological safeguards you may wish to undertake.

Information Security 101

You'll recall from chapters 2 and 6 that, for all the technological advancements we've made, threat agents still rely a lot on old-fashioned human failings to get their nasty work done. Education, awareness and security policies are the most effective safeguards for countering social engineering and other tricks.

The first step in Internet security is to train yourself, your family, and your staff in the safe and proper use of e-mail and the Internet. You will recall my misfortune when a colleague hit "Reply All" on one of my e-mail messages and thus sent it out to people I hadn't intended to receive it. Such a mishap can occur when people have not been trained in the use of e-mail. Too often, managers assume their staff know how to use a new tool, or they simply can't be bothered to show them how. Embarrassment to you and your company is only one possible result of such a lackadaisical approach.

When you first got your computer or first hooked it up to the Internet, you were probably so eager to play with your new toy or so busy with work that you didn't read your software manual thoroughly. Now that you are more familiar with your computer and the software you use, take some time to read through the manuals completely. You may be delighted to discover functions you never realized were available. Among these may be options that could improve your Internet security. "How-to" books for your particular operating system and software programs can also alert you to risky practices and useful security functions.

Procedures and Practices

Before you go out and purchase a security gadget, it pays to modify your operating practices on the Internet. There are some procedures you can implement that will substantially reduce the exposure of your computing environment to cyber threats.

First of all, you should establish a policy for accepted use of e-mail and the Internet in your home and at work. If you don't want your teenagers or your staff to visit certain types of sites on the Net, say so. You may wish to put your policy in print and have those using your computer system sign it. This will emphasize that they must take computer security as seriously as you do.

Devise policies and procedures for dealing with non-computer security issues. Internal network names, e-mail addresses and phone numbers should not be advertised. Often hackers armed with a little insider knowledge of these things can use it to raise their legitimacy and place themselves in a more advantageous position of trust in order to fool the user. A little knowledge can be a dangerous thing, facilitating an intrusion of major proportions.

Physical access to components of your computer system should be carefully controlled. Make users responsible for the computers they use, especially laptops that they take off-site. You may wish to consider establishing some sort of fine for loss of or damage to company-owned computers. This may help remind users to take extra care with their machines.

Often in smaller companies, there is no one to turn to when a computer problem arises. If you can't afford to have an information technology specialist on your staff, at least find one, preferably two, staff members with an interest in computers to act as system administrators. Give them the time and training to make sure the basic computer security precautions are being followed. If you are moving towards e-commerce, where you will be relying on the Internet to do transactions, take security into consideration when developing your business and financial plans.

What's the Password?

Passwords are the keys to your information. They are used in a variety of places:

1. Your computer can be configured with a boot-up password that is stored in firmware. A log-in prompt would be the first thing you will see when you turn on your computer, before the operating system loads. This effectively prevents anyone from hacking in. To do so, they would have to open up your computer and remove the battery sustaining the firmware memory, physically zeroizing it.

2. The next layer of password protection is at the operating system level where you would be prompted for access (account name and password) before you could do anything on the system.

3. The third check could be configured to occur when you request a network connection. The computer can check your access credentials (password) before letting you talk to the network.

4. Your Internet service provider will require that you (or an automated script) submit a valid account name and password combination.

5. The other place where you are likely to be challenged for an account and password is conducting businesses from Web sites on the Internet, like online shopping sites.

6. A screen saver password is a good idea if you work in an open office environment and have to leave your computer unattended for a short time. You should log off for longer absences or when you leave for the day.

Choose your passwords carefully. Passwords should not consist of words in English (or any language) or common proper names. Phrases like "open sesame" or "password" or "god" are examples of poor choices. It takes no time for a cracker using a computer to try every known word in a language including common given and surnames.

Different systems have different requirements for passwords. Some have set minimums and maximums for the number of characters a password must contain. Some do not allow certain types of characters to be used. But in general, a good password has several characteristics: it is longer than eight random characters; it includes at least one capital letter, one number, and one special character; and it does not represent an easy pattern on the keyboard. Here's an example of a good password:

9Evp6Qt@s

The longer a password is used, the greater the likelihood it has been compromised. Therefore, passwords should be changed regularly — at least once a year and also when there is a change in the circumstances of its use, such as when an employee leaves or moves to a new job. All passwords should be changed immediately if a security breach is suspected.

Often a Web site will ask you to establish a special account with them to proceed with a transaction, shop, or download information. The site may ask you to make up a password for this purpose. Do not use the same password that you have set up on your computer or use to gain access to your dial-up Internet account. This password and account name is often stored in your cookie file, which can be visible to all sites you visit on the Internet thereafter. Also, there is no guarantee that this password will be safeguarded at the Web site. If, for whatever reason, this password is compromised, you do not want it to be the same as your dial-up password or network password.

Your computer, network, and dial-up Internet account passwords are secret and only you should know them. Never give them away or reuse them. Do not give your password out to anyone, even the ISP or police; neither need your password for legitimate purposes.

Password Tips

- Keep your password secret.
- Do not give your password to anyone else, even if they seem to have a legitimate reason for it.
- Avoid using passwords you need to write down.
- Do not use the same password for more than one purpose.
- Change passwords at least once a year. Make this a component of your security plan.
- Change passwords when an employee leaves or changes jobs.
- Use at least eight characters in your password.
- Use screensaver passwords on terminals that may run unattended.

Password "Recipes":

- Use a misspelled word, e.g., sooprstarr.
- Add non-letters such as punctuation characters and numbers (if system permits), e.g., s00p!rstarr.
- Take a favorite phrase or adage and make it into an acronym, e.g., "don't count your chickens before they are hatched" becomes "dcycbtah".
- Mix upper and lower case letters, numbers, and punctuation, e.g., dCyC!6tah.
- Remove all vowels from a short phrase, e.g., short but sweet = shrtbtswt.
- Use a license plate–style pun, e.g., gr8sk8tR

What Not to Use for a Password:

- all blanks
- all numbers
- repeating characters or patterns (e.g., "zzzzzzzz" or "abababab")
- words that can be found in dictionaries
- dictionary words spelled backwards
- your login name

How's Your Browser?

Hackers delight in looking for security holes in popular browsers like Internet Explorer and Netscape. And, regrettably, they're often successful. The company that makes your browser software (which may also include your e-mail function) should have a Web site on which they post virus advisories and offer security patches and software updates for downloading. You or someone on your staff should make a habit of visiting your browser's Web site regularly for the latest security information.

Install the latest Internet browser with the latest security patches on your computer. Often the security holes in older versions have been fixed, and now all you will have to live with is the new ones. There is a saving grace period where new holes have yet to be discovered and hacker exploit scripts written. By staying ahead of the game, you cast yourself as an evolving or, at least, moving target.

Now that you are running the latest version of your browser and e-mail programs, it is important that you restrain their promiscuity. Browsers are shipped with maximum functionality and minimum security default settings. At the risk of sounding flippant, these programs want to talk to everyone about everything.

It is important to decide whether you prefer security to functionality. Personally, I keep my Web browser and e-mail secured as much as possible and open only for exceptions. To do this, you will have to change the options on your Web browser and e-mail applications manually.

(NOTE: Please bear in mind that browser versions may vary and the following is meant only as a general guide. I suggest that you consult your manual and "Help" menu when changing security-related options.)

These suggestions should close the majority of Web-based vulnerabilities:

Open your Web browser and find "Internet Options" from one of the pull-down menus (usually "Tools"). There should be several tabs offering additional options. Beside many of these option is a box which can be toggled (checked on or off) with a mouse click.

The "Wallet" feature stores Internet shopping information like your credit card number. Feel free to remove any information you do not wish to appear over the Internet.

From the "Advanced" tag there are some more settings you may wish to consider. I suggest that you begin by toggling the check box using the mouse to

» disable script debugging;
» disable install on demand; and
» uncheck or disable all Java boxes.

In the "Security" sub-section:

» enable the check for revocation;
» pick "do not save encrypted files to disk";
» empty temporary Internet files when browser is closed;
» use SSL 3.0 and TLS only and disable fortezza, PCT and SSL 2.0 use; and
» enable warning messages.

All this fiddling may seem daunting to the average user. An alternative that is nearly as effective is to just select the "Maximum" security setting from the main "Internet Options: General" tab, and reset to "Medium" wherever there is a particular and trusted Web site you wish to interact with.

Travel Advice for the Information Highway

Here are some thoughts to ponder when you are surfing the Web, posting to newsgroups, taking part in chats, or filling in forms online: Every time you use the Internet, you are giving clues about your identity, preferences, thoughts, likes, and dislikes. Even trivial information can be injurious once amassed. Everything you see on your computer screen or type into a Web page form can conceivably be viewed on computers along the path between the Web server and your computer.

Earlier, I discussed notions of privacy on the Internet and how some people take it very seriously, while others don't. If you do care about protecting your privacy online, you should first of all be cautious about anything you type and send over the Internet, whether it is an e-mail message, a Web form, or a posting to a chat room. Remember that what you type can persist for a long time in computer memory and that once you release it you have very little control over who reads it.

Besides the content of your Web communications, there are parties out there who are interested in where you go when you wander the Web. If you don't want to be followed on your Web travels, you have to actively cover your steps, because many browsers and Web sites have been programmed to keep track of your journey.

One step you can take is to regularly purge your cache and Internet history files. The intent of these files is to speed up the process of displaying regularly visited Web sites by storing the elements of these Web pages on your computer in a place called a "cache." The idea of the cache if used exclusively for this purpose is not a bad one. The problem is that it also provides a record of everywhere you have been, what you have read, or what you have written on the Web. It is possible, given the right circumstances, for strangers to retrieve your Internet history from your computer's cache and use it for their own profit.

I discussed cookies earlier. These are little files some Web sites place on your computer when you visit them. Again, their ostensible purpose is to speed up your

Web Surfing Safety Tips

- Only download programs from sites you trust.
- Don't allow children to use the Internet without supervision.
- Set clear policies for appropriate Internet use at home and at work.
- If you share your computer system with others, consider using filter programs for blocking access to potentially dangerous or offensive Web sites.
- Be careful about giving out personal information in public forums or on corporate Web site forms.
- Use an up-to-date version of your browser software.
- Manually set browser options, such as acceptance of cookies and Java applets, to an appropriate level of security for your situation.
- Clear your cache after each Web browsing session.
- Look for privacy statements and seals on the sites before filling in a Web form

Web Shopping:

- Use your credit card rather than checks or money orders to make Internet purchases — they offer some recourse in the event of a dispute.

- Check for security measures on the site, such as encryption level (click on the lock in the lower corner) before entering any personal information such as credit card number or banking information.

- Look for additional contact information on the site, such as a street address and phone number.

- Read the return policy, particularly for downloaded items such as software.

- Make sure all costs (shipping, handling, insurance, customs, etc.) are included in the final quoted price.

- Print out a copy of the purchase form and any special information such as returns policy and delivery instructions. Put the date of purchase on it and keep it for your records in case of a dispute.

access to their site and to compile marketing information, but they can also be used in more intrusive ways that you may not approve of — if you knew about them. Browser software often has a default setting to accept cookies, but you should be able to turn this off in the "Internet options" or "Preferences" menus. You should also delete cookie files that may have inadvertently been copied to your system. Normally these can be found within your Web browser folder on your hard drive under the names

c:\temp

c:\windows\temp

c:\windows\cookies

c:\windows\history

If you feel uncomfortable doing this, then it's best to leave it alone, but keep in mind that a record of your browsing experience is being recorded.

Finally, be careful where you surf. Do not go to places that you know are bad. If you are frequenting seedy underground haunts within cyberspace on a regular basis, your risk of picking something unpleasant up is much higher.

E-Mailing with Confidence

E-mail is one of the most popular and useful Internet functions, and has been quickly adopted by even the most computer phobic. But because it is so easy to use, people don't think twice about it — and they should. E-mails have been used in court cases, been the instigationfor lawsuits and firings, and have caused embarrassment to those who didn't think twice before pressing the "Send" button. Scam artists have also found it an ideal tool for finding new victims to prey on. It has also proven to be a great carrier for computer viruses.

One simple preventive measure can limit your exposure to many of these ills: do not use e-mail to transmit sensitive information. If you do want to use e-mail for this purpose, use encryption. Many of the latest versions of popular e-mail programs offer this function.

When using e-mail for business purposes, use the same formal language as you would for other types of business correspondence. Remember that e-mail is not as ephemeral as it seems; your message may live long in cyberspace, and be read by others besides the intended recipient.

Do careful research before collecting e-mail addresses and using them for commercial purposes. Advise customers if you intend to put their e-mail address on a mailing list. Give them the option not to have their address placed on the list. You probably do not want to damage your image by being labeled a "spammer." Also, keep up with legislation regarding the use of e-mail addresses for commercial purposes, such as the Children's Online Privacy Protection Act, to ensure you are in compliance.

As for dangerous incoming e-mails, these can be limited by being careful when giving out your e-mail address. If you use e-mail for many different types of correspondence, have a different e-mail address for each type — one for free registration on Web sites, one for posting on your favorite newsgroup, one for entering online contests, and so on. Keep one or two addresses that you use solely for important correspondence, and give these out sparingly.

Read sender and subject lines carefully before opening e-mail, and don't open unexpected attachments, even if they appear to be from a reliable source. Recent viruses were able to disguise themselves in e-mail attachments sent from apparently legitimate users.

E-Mail Tips

- Read manuals before using your e-mail program.
- Learn to use your e-mail program's security options, such as filters and encryption.
- Take care when opening e-mail attachments, especially from unknown sources.
- Scan an e-mail attachment with anti-virus software before opening it.
- Where possible, send and receive text documents in the body of the e-mail message rather than as attachments.
- Use "disposable" e-mail addresses for posting to online forums such as chat rooms and message boards.
- Reserve one e-mail address for private and sensitive correspondence only.
- Don't give out your e-mail address — on Web forms, for instance — without knowing how it is going to be used.
- Double-check the e-mail address before pressing "Send."
- Send "spam" e-mails directly to the trash bin — do not reply to them, do not pass them along to your friends, do not buy the products or services offered.
- Avoid sending sensitive information by e-mail. If transmitting sensitive information, such as your credit card number, by e-mail, use encryption.
- Use anonymous remailers to protect your privacy.
- Teach your children how to use e-mail safely.

Business E-mail

- Give your staff training in use of the e-mail system.
- Ask permission before sending promotional e-mails or adding customers' e-mail addresses to an e-mailing list used for marketing purposes.
- Treat business e-mails as you would other business correspondence — use business-like language.
- When sending muliple copies of an e-mail, use the BCC (blind carbon copy) rather than the CC option to protect recipients' addresses.
- Do not use the e-mail system to discuss security issues.

Check your e-mail program or service for filtering, blocking and sorting options. These can help limit the amount of junk e-mail you receive. Some "spam" will likely still get through. Do not respond to the sender, even to complain, as this is merely a way of confirming that there's a real live person at your address, making you a target for even more spam.

Contingency Plans and Reaction

It is always wise to hope for the best but plan for the worst. This is where contingency planning and disaster recovery come into play. If, in spite of all your precautions, you do experience some sort of computer disaster, whether due to an accident or human error, or through a deliberate, malicious attack, you should have some strategies in place to minimize its effects.

If you rely on your computer system, e-mail, and the Internet for day-to-day business operations, you will need to work out a step-by-step plan for dealing with different types of threat events, and for limiting or repairing any damage inflicted by them. There are formal methods for establishing a plan, and you may need to enlist the help of a professional in applying them to your situation.

Again, the elements you decide to include in your plan depend on an assessment of your risk. Business users may need quite extensive plans carefully described in their policy and procedures manual. For most of us at home, however, our plan will probably not need to be very elaborate. Some of the threats to home users I've discussed parallel those in the real world and we already know how we would handle them if they came to pass. For example, if you buy something over the Internet using your credit card and never receive the item, you would complain to the seller and perhaps to your credit card company. Or if a stranger approaches your child over the Internet, you would go to the police about it and keep your child away from the computer until the danger has been dealt with.

However, one disaster most home computer users are often unprepared for is the loss of data stored on their computer. We often don't realize how much information we have on our home computers until we lose it. Financial records, health records, calendars and schedules, correspondence, family photos, artwork, novels-in-progress, browser bookmarks . . . There may not be a direct financial cost tied to loss of these materials but the emotional impact can be great. You may recall the news story a few years back of a well-known actress who apparently suffered a nervous collapse when the computer files for the book she had been working on were erased from her computer.

While this may be an extreme response to data loss, at the very least it would be annoying to have to re-input all your information into your computer. It is sometimes possible to recover lost or damaged files from a hard drive that has been erased by a virus or some accidental activity, but it may require the costly skills of an expert to do it. There is a fairly simple way to avoid these situations, however: keep copies of all your files and update them on a regular basis, or "back up."

Backing Up

Most computer users have had at least one data-loss incident severe enough to impress on them the need for backups. But like most humans, they do one backup following an incident, put the disks somewhere, and that's it. This is why we need to devise a solid backup strategy. This will include determining

» the frequency and extent of the backup,
» the backup method,
» the medium to use, and
» where backed-up files will be stored.

How often files are backed up and which files need to be backed up will depend on how much you use your computer and how reliant you are on the data it contains. The backup procedure has to be convenient or it probably won't get done. The medium used for storing backed-up files must balance considerations of convenience and budget. The backup files have to be kept safe but also easily accessible if restoration is ever needed. The restoration procedure should also be straightforward and speedy; most users will want to get back to work quickly after a disruption.

A good guideline for determining backup frequency is to look at how often substantial changes are made to computer data. If you work at your computer every day, you might want to make a daily back up. If you use your computer once a week to do your finances, then you may only have to back up following a work session.

This guideline can also apply when deciding which files to back up. Backing up everything on your computer every day would take a lot of time and a lot of storage, so you will probably have different backup schedules for different files, depending on how valuable they are to you and how often changes are made to them.

The simplest backup method is to copy a file directly to some portable medium, such as a floppy disk. This is easy and direct, but can get tedious if you have many files to copy. Fortunately, many software programs come equipped with a backup utility program that is easy to use and allows you to specify which files you want to backup, then automates the copying process for you. They also can help in the process of restoring files after a crash.

Common media for making backups are floppy disks (1.4M storage), Zip drives (100–250M), CD-ROMs (650M), and digital linear tape (DLT). Floppy disks have limited storage space, CD-ROMs are more of a permanent storage solution, and DLT is reserved for large networks that need oodles of storage space and are worth the investment in the technology. For the average user or small business, Zip drives and disks or re-writeable CD-ROMs offer the best options.

Whatever medium you use, the backed-up files should be stored in a safe location, preferably away from your computer. (If some physical disaster like a flood destroys your computer, you don't want the backups lost along with it.) Also, if the medium is magnetic (diskettes and tapes) you will want a storage location away from electrical and magnetic sources. A fireproof filing cabinet that can be locked might be a good option. Business users may want to consider secure off-site storage.

Incident Handling

When deliberate threat actions overcome existing protection schemes, where do you turn and who do you call? A good place to start is the trouble shooting manual, to ascertain that the effect is not accidental. If you have tried various suggestions without success, or strongly suspect that you are the victim of a deliberate Internet-based attack, call your Internet service provider. Most ISPs have abuse, help, or technical assistance phone lines. The majority of network-based threat incidents like spamming or probing can be handled at this level.

If it is at all possible, do not communicate by e-mail if you suspect the attacker has compromised your system — you do not want to give the threat agents a potential means to monitor the progress of your investigation into their activities.

The next stage for larger enterprises or major incidents is to contact a computer emergency response team (CERT). Consult the Forum for Incident Response and Security Teams (FIRST) Web site (www.first.org) to determine which CERT you should report to and keep this information handy. For example, CANCERT handles incidents in Canada, AUSCERT in Australia, and CERT/CC takes calls from all over the U.S.A. Note that within the U.S.A. there are many CERTs; there may be one more suited to your geographical or business sector. Again, use the phone rather than e-mail to report a serious incident.

FIRST is an international coalition of vulnerability analysts and computer incident response teams from governments and the private sector. CERT missions vary, but typically they include the following:

> » Provide accurate and timely and trusted security information;
> » Increase awareness of networked computer threats;
> » Handle incidents;
> » Provide limited technical assistance;
> » Correlate activities at your site with others;
> » Give early warning of attacks;
> » Contact other sites involved in the incident directly or indirectly; and
> » Liaise with law enforcement.

Basic Information

When you report an incident to a CERT you will be asked to provide some information to help resolve the incident. The data may be used to compile statistics and issue advisories to the greater community after your sensitive site information has been sanitized from the report. Typical data a CERT requires include:

» contact information;
» what was affected;
» the time zone, time, and date, and how accurate they are;
» extracts of system logs;
» restrictions you wish to apply on information;
» past incidents and actions; and
» an explanation of what you want done (information only, coordination with external sites, a cease of the actions, evidence for prosecution, a report, or protection advice.)

What to Do in the Meantime

You should be concerned about what we call "business resumption" after an attack on your network or a virus infection. The first step is to assess how bad the situation is and ask yourself if you can work through it or if you have to suspend computer operations.

Indecision at this juncture is in fact a decision to do nothing — this is the worst choice. If the situation warrants and you must turn off the computers and call for help, then it is best that you do it right away and set in motion a contingency plan for continuing operations without computers. The first part of every plan should clearly specify the conditions under which you would make the decision to shut things down or to keep the computers running and work through a disruption. For example, a widespread virus infection may require that you quarantine your computers — not let your employees near them until you have things fixed. On the other hand, an intrusion by a hacker may only require that you sever Internet connections until you can patch things up; meanwhile, your employees may be able to work.

The contingency plan also needs to specify decision points in time; for example, if your computers are down for more than four hours, then you'll revert to paper-based operations. Without time limits on decisions, your staff could be waiting indefinitely for their computers to come up and never resort to alternative means of getting their work done, thus adding to the damage through loss of productivity.

According to CERT/CC, compromised machines must be disconnected from the network, their drives wiped, and the OS reinstalled from clean media. Watch for reintroduction of malicious code (the problem) in the data restored from backups. Finally, sensitive information like passwords needs to be changed.

Handling the Intrusion

If the computer problem you are having is due to a hacking incident, there are some additional things you should do. You will need to preserve logs as evidence should you ever wish to prosecute. These logs will also come in handy in resolving the incident with your ISP or CERT. These logs can be generated automatically by your firewall, intrusion detection systems, or operating system. Even the error messages are helpful. Do not forget the exact time that events occurred. The first step in resolving the incidents will be to coordinate your time and the network time with universal time. Keep notes on evidence handling, including witnesses. If it ever comes to court, the veracity of the data will be questioned if there are lapses in the way the evidence was collected and handled. Essentially, you will have to prove that no one could have reasonably altered the data or made it up.

However, the chances of a successful prosecution for these incidents are slight because the legal profession is still operating for the most part in the industrial age — the laws cannot be interpreted or rewritten fast enough to account for what is possible in cyberspace. Generally speaking, it is not worth the effort of pursuing these cases through the courts unless you can recover large sums of money or have a legal department with some time on their hands. For most of us, the relatively easy and sufficient recourse is to get the hackers' account suspended and have them blacklisted with ISPs.

Chapter 10
Configuring for Self Defense

Once you have modified your basic practices of Internet use to include safe surfing, e-mail precautions, and strong password protection, there are additional technological measures you can take to protect your computing environment. You lock your office doors at night. If you are serious about security, you have a monitored alarm system. But do you do the same for your computer network?

Static security mechanisms in a computer system are analogous to door locks and window bars on your house or place of business. At face value, they act as a deterrent, warding off would-be attackers. Intrinsically, they frustrate, minimize or slow down an attack. To be effective, protection devices must be placed near system vulnerabilities. The reasoning is that you may not know much about the attacker but you are aware of where you are most vulnerable. A football helmet is a safeguard designed to protect your head, regardless of which team you may be playing against.

Many of the measures I discuss here require more technical knowledge than you may possess to put into place. The idea here is to give an overview of the more technological aspects of computer security so that you can better evaluate your needs and prepare yourself to discuss them with a computer security specialist.

Virus Scanners and E-mmunity

Viruses and other malicious code most frequently slip in through e-mail attachments and diskettes. The solution is to install virus-scanning software and keep it updated every month by downloading the latest libraries from the vendor over the Internet. This will ensure that your scanner will recognize and eradicate the newest viruses.

A virus scanner works several basic ways: it scans for changes in important files on your computer (files that should not be modified). It also periodically scans your hard drive for telltale virus activity. It can be set to check out any new program or file loaded on your systems, and be forced to scan a diskette of a particular file that you suspect as being a high risk.

Remember that with viruses, file names mean nothing. Malicious code can be made to look like anything or can live within a legitimate host. Trojan programs to date have required an *.exe* file extension so that they can be activated with a double click or "run" command, but doubtless there's a hacker somewhere out there working industriously to write one that can launch on its own.

There are more and more virus scares on the Net. Many of them are hoaxes that are propagated through chain mail. Precautionary shutdowns of your business operations are not the answer. You must mount an effective self-denial attack. Should you catch a virus, do not panic! Often people do more harm in a panic than the virus could even achieve. Do not reformat your hard drive. Buy the latest virus-scanning software and "e-noculate" yourself, and do not forget to scan your backups before you reinstall your applications and data.

Content with Content

Whether you are an employer concerned about employees trafficking salacious material or a parent worried about what your kids will see on the Net, there are software utilities that can filter information in and out of your computing environment by recognizing key words like "sex" or "xxx" or "games." The latest Web browsers will allow a certain level of filtering already, configurable from the options menu.

Think carefully before installing filters on your home or business computer system. First of all, they are not yet perfect, and some legitimate traffic may get blocked along with the bad stuff. Conversely, they may not block everything you wish to have blocked. Those really determined to break through filtering programs will find a way to do it.

Secondly, filters may have an adverse psychological effect. For parents, a filter may provide a false sense of security if they think it means they no longer need to supervise their kids' Internet activities. At some point the kids may figure out how to outwit the filter, or simply go somewhere else to use a filterless machine. The filter is not a substitute for teaching safe surfing practices or supervising online activities. For older kids and for employees, using a filter may send the message that you do not trust them, which can create a negative atmosphere.

Firewalls

A firewall is a specific protective safeguard used to regulate communications to and from your computer or network. A firewall acts very much like a traffic cop standing in an intersection. The cop directs packets of cars like the firewall controls the flow of information packets — making sure the packets do not go somewhere they are not supposed to. Just as the cop may want to stop traffic from entering a private residential street, you may similarly want to restrict access to sensitive areas of your computer.

We can draw a parallel with the roads of the real world with virtual ports in a computer communication channel. Every computer has an Internet protocol (IP) address assigned either permanently or temporarily for the period of time you are on a network or the Internet. These IP addresses are like your civic address: house number, street name and postal code. A port is like a sub-address much like the attention line in a letter (e.g., 5555 Main Street, Ottawa, Ontario, Canada, K1P 4G6 Attention: Sales Department.)

There are 64,000 possible ports or sub addresses associated with every Internet protocol address. Some ports have been assigned, by consensus, for common Internet services such as e-mail, file transfer, and Web sites. For example, IP address 207.46.138.11 and port 80 correspond to a Microsoft Web service address. The vast majority of ports have not been assigned. For something like Web traffic, temporary or ephemeral ports are assigned randomly from one of the available high-numbered ports (like #56789) to accommodate information flow back and forth between the client and the server on the Web.

A firewall is an important safeguard to a network or client-side computer because they regulate how traffic enters and leaves your computing environment based upon rules you have established. In reality, a firewall can be a stand-alone computer dedicated to this purpose or just a piece of software that runs on your PC and operates between your applications and the external connection to the Internet. They can cost as little as $100 and upwards of $150,000. Cost is driven by their capability to filter a larger quantity of traffic with better resolution.

By default, firewalls with no established rules block all traffic from moving between (entering or exiting) your environment and the Internet. The most basic rules would specify what type of traffic is permitted to travel, in what direction, on what ports. For example, you may establish a rule the allows e-mail to be received and sent using the standard port (number 25). By default, if it is not explicitly allowed it is forbidden, and therefore someone trying to retrieve a file through another port would be blocked. More sophisticated (and expensive) firewalls can set even more precise rules; for example, they may only permit files to be sent using an authorized application through an unique port to a specific address during work hours.

The average computer user can install personal firewall software on their system for about $100. Unlike their expensive stand-alone counterparts, specifying rules on a personal firewall is easy as pie. Initially, after installation all ports are closed. You then would attempt to connect to the Internet and carry on as you would regularly. You are prompted by the firewall software each time some application wishes to communicate out or in from an external site, for a decision. Do you wish this application to communicate? If you say yes then a rule is established to permit this type of traffic and application from then on. Conversely, if you are not doing anything in particular on the Internet and some application you do not recognize from the outside or on your own computer wants to communicate, the firewall software will stop it and ask for a decision. Should you say no, this type of communication will be blocked without bothering you. The firewall will keep a log of all the unknown and blocked traffic for you. It can make for scary reading when you see how many suspicious or illicit connection attempts are made on your system.

The most basic type of firewall acts as a circuit gateway, in that it establishes a straight connection between the external (Internet) and internal (computing) domains. Again, this firewall acts just like the traffic cop who regulates the direction of traffic and who may even discriminate between types of packets and routes, for example, stopping cars from driving in bus lanes or large trucks from using residential roads. But the traffic cop does not usually look inside each vehicle and verify that the contents are terrorists with a truck full of fertilizer. Likewise, a firewall of this type does not examine the content of the packets. If the header (external appearance) appears correct, it will pass the packet right through to a valid destination.

The next level of sophistication in firewalls would examine the packet as it appears at the external interface and if it passes inspection would make a copy of it available at the internal interface. This is like calling a doctor's office after hours and asking to speak with the doctor directly. Their office will likely not release the doctor's home phone number or extension. Instead, the staff will probably vet your information, copy it down, and pass a note on. You have no doubt seen another example at airport security. People arriving in wheelchairs are transferred to an airline chair before proceeding through the checkpoint. This prevents hidden packages from slipping through. Airport security checkpoints also use x-ray machines and metal detectors to examine the contents that pass this external-internal boundary.

Some firewalls have what are called "application proxies" that act as data brokers. They do not allow direct communication between the Internet and your computer. Furthermore, well-written proxies verify that what is arriving and leaving on the e-mail port looks and feels like a real e-mail. Any attacks against your system are stopped at the firewall. If the attack is severe enough, it may crash your firewall. Well-designed firewalls "fail closed." This means if they crash, they shut all ports off, barring all access.

Firewalls do have their limitations, however. They do not detect application-layer attacks like malicious code, viruses or harmful applets if they are packaged within a legitimate traffic type, just as in the real world a traffic cop is unlikely to notice a terrorist on a city bus as it passes by. A perfectly secure firewall is one that is not connected, but of course this is impractical. The biggest mistake people make when installing a firewall is to set rules that are too permissive, ones that let anything through. This is like putting locks on your doors but leaving the key in the lock. A properly installed firewall is a good idea and is a big step towards improved security, but there is still more that can be done.

The Next Steps:
Detection and Response

Modifying online operating practices, configuring your operating system and Web browser security settings, and installing a virus checker and a personal firewall are likely sufficient measures for the average home user to mitigate online risks. If you are running a business and have much more to lose, you may want to take the next few steps in security. These involve installing more complicated and usually more expensive programs. You will also want to have more formal and rigorous risk assessment and risk management plans.

The reality of security is that many people install a high-grade lock on their door, but then leave their windows open. Security must be well balanced. Remember, the threat will follow the path of least resistance, like water pouring over low points and in through cracks. For more complex computing environments, sound security engineering practices ought to be followed. I would strongly suggest hiring a qualified professional information technology security engineer to review your architecture.

Prevention and protection act only as deterrents or minor impediments to a crime. Most businesses and many homes have monitored alarm systems in addition to locks. But unless the police are alerted when the alarm goes off, thieves could still achieve their aim. The threat agent could conceivably take as long as required to break in if there is no response to the attack. For security to be effective there must be a system not only for detection but for effective response as well.

There are devices and software for computers that detect compromise attempts and failures in protection mechanisms. Unlike static protection systems like firewalls, these detection and response systems act dynamically to counter threat actions. Some do this in real time. The most common tool of this type is the intrusion detection system.

Intrusion Detection Systems (IDS)

An intrusion detection system (IDS) for computers performs much like a car alarm, but with more options. It detects break-ins or potentially harmful activities and reacts in a variety of ways depending on your needs. Anomalies are detected and logged for later review and analysis by security. Activities by that threat source can be immediately blocked. In some cases this is accomplished by having the IDS establish a new temporary rule on the firewall or packet filtering router. An alarm can be generated and a message (voice, pager, or e-mail) can be sent to the system administrator warning of any incursions. Tracing activities can begin on the source of the trouble automatically, or the system can be programmed to counter strike at the source. This setup is called a "Blitzkrieg" server. However, it is not recommended because an attacker can use this automated response to fool the system into attacking another site.

There are several different intrusion detection systems on the market. Setting them up, optimizing them to reduce false positive alarms, and interpreting the results is a non-trivial exercise best left to professionals. One option is to sub-contract the monitoring of your network to a trusted third party, just as many companies do with their physical security requirements. An IDS is more than the average user needs.

Operational Assurance

Operational assurance is like your yearly regular checkup by your doctor. Not only do the qualified technicians tap, prod, and poke, but their assessment typically involves interviewing and counseling on a healthy computing lifestyle. If your computing environment is large enough, there is merit in having this kind of checkup. Operational assurance can provide confidence that security needs are being satisfied.

Operational assurance is obtained through an analysis of real-world evidence, including a security posture assessment, audit, architecture design review, and regular security testing in an operational setting. Each one of these processes can be accurately benchmarked and incrementally improved.

An important part of the technical security assessment of a computing environment is obtained through penetration testing, ethical hacking or, to be more politically correct, security posture assessment and vulnerability-testing analysis.

A professional assessment may use a variety of automated tools (Cybercop, ISS Security Scanner) and some specialized software and hardware to test all aspects of your systems in a methodical way. The process usually includes a security engineering analysis of your architecture and a detailed interpretation of the results. The final report should contain specific vulnerability descriptions explaining the significance of each finding in the context of your computing and business environment. The report will likely explain how to remedy each exposure. Also, the non-technical security measures discussed in chapter 9 are just as important to a computing environment and need to be addressed at some point within operational assurance.

Choosing the Right Person for the Job

Many enterprises pay hackers to break into their systems and trust them to fix the problem. Not a wise move! Beware of whom you employ to do your security assessment. Do not trust amateur hackers or self-proclaimed security experts to do this, for two reasons: one, they are not qualified, and two, they lack an assurance of trust.

Typically, these amateurs run an automated program like SATAN against your system, hand you the printout, and send you a bill for a few thousand dollars. Nice work if you can get it. This is like hiring a high school student to tell you your blood pressure, pulse, height, and weight for a thousand dollars and then calling it a complete physical. If these individuals were so good at hacking, then it stands to reason they would be able to make a legitimate living at it as information technology professionals.

Reputable information technology security professionals, like doctors, teachers, and chartered accountants, have recognized qualifications, skills, and experience within the field. However, the pool of "security experts" is rife with charlatans. Here are some things you should look for on a résumé before hiring someone to conduct a penetration test on your network:

1. A degree in electrical, computer engineering or computer science from a recognized university or college;
2. Status or eligibility as a professional engineer;
3. Specialization in computer or information systems security;
4. Recognition or certification by a professional IT security association such as Certified Information Systems Security Professional (CISSP);
5. Three to five years' experience working in the field;
6. Appropriate experience and skill set for your requirements;
7. List of past projects and clients;
8. Security clearance, enhanced reliability check, or bonded status;
9. QA standards like ISO 9000;
10. Company is registered;
11. Company is recognized by the National Security Agency (NSA) in the U.S. or Communications Security Establishment (CSE) in Canada or national IT security authority of another country;
12. References.

Making Secure E-Commerce a Reality

Having a corporate Web site for advertising and customer relations purposes is one thing; using the site to sell your products or services directly over the Internet involves a higher level of risk. In the former case, most of the cyber threats amount to inconvenient annoyances. In e-commerce, however, there is the real risk of serious harm being done to your company and your customers' finances and privacy. If you are contemplating a move to e-commerce, security considerations must form a part of your business and financial planning.

There are two places where secure transactions are required for the average online purchase. They are between you and the merchant, and between the merchant and the bank (credit card company). Credit cards, computers, Web browsers, and cryptography are the four components that make all this happen.

In today's wired world everything is connected at some point. If you want to buy something you can go to the store, or mail order the old-fashioned way by telephone or post. Similarly, you can order nearly anything over the Internet. Regardless of how you pay, the transaction will likely go over the Internet at some point. If you use an automated teller machine to get cash, it performs the necessary debt transaction over the Internet (albeit on a virtual private network). If you pay the cashier with a credit card or debit card, then the transaction moves from the store's card reader device over the Internet to the main banking computers. These systems use specialized devices, dedicated or dial-up circuits, and virtual private networks running particular protocols. They are intended to provide better security than regular e-mail. Yet, the Internet is omnipresent and extends into these domains.

Ordering products off of the Internet is nearly the same from a security perspective as the way you and I have traditionally done business. The one big exception is that the Internet allows a large variety of methods for conducting commercial transactions; some of them are safe and others are not so safe. The banking community put in place an infrastructure for the use of debt and credit cards, one in which security provisions were well thought out. There are risks but these have been calculated and managed by these financial institutions in terms of the business domain. Moreover, they do indemnify the user against loss through fraudulent acts.

Things are a little less certain when it comes to Internet-based e-commerce, owing to the reliance on multipurpose hardware, software and network connections. In other words, we have migrated from conducting our business using private facilities designed specifically for this role to using a general-purpose, public infrastructure.

You can purchase an item from a merchant by sending them an e-mail with your credit card number and its expiry date. The merchant in turn can submit the transaction manually (either using a device or by paper). The transaction can be successfully refuted by you, the cardholder, because there is no signature on the transaction nor was the card manually swiped. The merchant assumes the majority of the risk in credit card transactions. You, on the other hand, may have your e-mail intercepted and credit card number stolen. The result is that you will be left with the aggravation of canceling your card and settling the affair with your credit card company's fraud department. There may be a $50 charge to you account for the pains the credit card company has to go to to make things better and send you a new card.

The challenge in e-commerce is how to use a free public infrastructure to conduct business in a simple, cost-effective, and secure manner — simple meaning that the average citizen can perform a "no hassle" online transaction with no help or training; cost effective meaning using existing facilities rather than developing and deploying special devices at the merchant's and client's locations; and secure meaning that the information can only be used by those with authorized access.

These challenges have been met by the Internet, with home computers replacing end-user devices providing the simplicity and cost effectiveness, and recent advances in public key cryptography providing the necessary security.

Secure Transactions

The word "secure" has a very specific meaning in the parlance of the professional security community when used in the context of computers and communications. A "secure" communication is one in which the properties of confidentiality, integrity, authenticity, and non-repudiation have been assured through the use of an approved crypto-system. A "secure" computer system not only uses the fore-mentioned cryptography but also is built from products endorsed by national cryptological authorities like the National Security Agency in the U.S.A. or approved labs. The operating systems used by a secure system have a trusted rating and the network itself has undergone a thorough certification and accreditation process that meets international standards.

The confidentiality property means that the information must be protected from eavesdropping. A threat agent may be able to intercept the communication but should not be able to read it. The level of protection that is applied should be enough to place the cost of exploitation beyond what most reasonable attackers are willing to spend. This level of protection constantly needs to be raised in order to keep pace with technological advances by the threat.

The other components of a secure transaction are to ensure that you are communicating with the right person. The authenticity of the information from both parties needs to be verified throughout the exchange. The integrity of the information needs to be preserved. Accidentally or deliberately corrupted data need to be detected and corrected by a secure system. Furthermore, evidence that the transaction occurred must be preserved so that neither party can refute that the deal took place. This is the property of non-repudiation.

Attributes of a secure system for e-commerce also include high reliability, availability, and accountability of its users for their transactions. Cryptography fills the guts of e-commerce.

Cryptography

I touched on cryptography and cryptanalysis earlier, and now I will go into a bit more technical detail. It's a very technical subject but having some understanding of how cryptography works will help you see how it can be integrated with the other secure components of e-commerce. If you are interested in the history of cryptography and cryptanalysis, I have listed some relevant books and Web sites in the Resource section at the back of this book.

Cryptography — the art of secret writing — has existed since the beginning of recorded time. Progressively more complex schemes have been developed for hiding the meaning of the information and making signatures or official seals harder to counterfeit. The science of steganography attempts to hide the existence of the message altogether by using things like invisible ink or embedding an electronic message into a graphical image on a Web page. In all cases, a key is required to unlock the hidden meaning or verify authenticity of the sender.

Modern-day cryptography is based upon mathematics, where large numbers are the keys. In a practical application, the mathematical mess is hidden from average users, who need only remember a password and address.

The question is, how do two people communicate securely over the Internet without someone else reading their mail? The answer is that the cryptography software converts your message into numbers, performs a mathematical operation on the numbers involving a secret number (key), and sends it along. You will need to ensure that the other party has the shared secret number (key) by some other way (phone message or courier), and that they know the mathematical operation you used to encipher your message. The other party takes your message and performs the reverse deciphering operation and ends up with the original text. All of this can be automated and ideally occurs transparently to the user.

The challenge for Internet engineers is to provide you with an acceptable level of protection in your Web-based interactions without you having to do a thing. Ease of use is a significant factor in increasing the use of cryptography. The downside is that it is not a trivial task to determine what your Web browser is doing when it comes to public key cryptography. Right now there are good and bad implementations of cryptography, both claiming to provide a secure communications session. The security community is pressuring the application programmers to adhere to best practices. The average user can only hope that the technical issues are sorted out behind the scenes in everyone's best interest.

All this is to say that many sites falsely claim to operate a secure computing environment. Do not take this claim as advertised without knowing the specifics. The good news is that flaws in the design of secure online systems are widely published. In the absence of any central and trusted authority to certify that a site meets best commercial standards, the average user needs to add some uncertainty into the assessment of any claim made by a site.

The trick to modern cryptography is that certain mathematical operations are easier to perform in one direction than in the reverse. It is essential that each party have the shared secret key prior to communicating. This use of keys is called "symmetric" because the same key is used by all parties to the conversation for both sending (enciphering) and receiving (deciphering) the message. However, key distribution can be a costly affair. In the military, couriers had to carry codes in briefcases handcuffed to their wrists. Many a courier was captured and codes compromised during the First and Second World Wars.

(I should note here that, strictly speaking, there are differences among the terms *encipherment, encryption, encoding,* and *secret writing,* but the distinction is not important for the average person wishing to use cryptography in a practical way.)

Symmetric key cryptography is still used in high-grade military communications systems that benefit from an existing key distribution infrastructure. The challenge for cryptographers has been to come up with a way whereby anyone can communicate securely with anyone else without having to previously exchange a shared secret and credentials (identification). Enter the world of public key cryptography.

Public Key Cryptography

Public key cryptography uses the property of "asymmetric" keys. One key locks (encrypts) the message while another separate key unlocks (decrypts) the message. One of these keys you always keep secret, the other you publish publicly. The actual algorithm is also public knowledge. We will skip the math. It is enough to say that some mathematical equations exhibit this property, and we now have a practical application for it. Large prime numbers are involved, but this is not important in understanding the basic concepts.

The exchange simply works as follows: Anyone wishing to send you a message takes the plaintext and encrypts it with your public key, and then sends it to you by e-mail. You would receive it and decrypt it using your secret key. Only you can read it because without knowledge of your secret key, breaking or reading the message is what mathematicians call a "hard problem." Conversely, a message such as a short digital signature (the electronic version of signing on the dotted line) that is encrypted with a secret key can be decrypted with a public key. As you may have gathered, the keys come in pairs, secret and public. You can also have two different sets of key pairs, one for signing things and one for encrypting the message.

Digital Signatures

For a long time, in our commercial, financial, and legal transactions, we have used our signatures to indicate our agreement and acceptance of terms described in documents. Handwritten signatures are widely regarded as nearly impossible to forge — faked signatures can usually be recognized by handwriting experts. No electronic equivalent of the written signature is yet in wide use. Various schemes have been proposed for online authentication, such as digitized thumbprints and retinal scans. But the digital signature appears to be the approach most likely to be widely adopted in e-commerce in the coming years. In spring 2000, U.S. president Bill Clinton signed a bill that made digital signatures legally binding.

We sign something to indicate intent. Our signature must be bound uniquely to our identity on the document we are signing. We cannot have someone forging our signature or lifting it off one document and placing it on another. But a digital signature is still just a bunch of numbers ultimately, so how is it secure? The way it works is that your signature for any given document is different, and no one but you can predict what it would be. However, others can still verify that it was you who did the signing. The basic concept is that it is much easier to read your signature than to write it. Asymmetric key cryptography plays a central role.

You will remember that you use someone's public key to encrypt a message sent to them and they in turn use their secret key to decrypt the message. The intent here is to hide the message from casual eavesdropping. Digital signatures are not concerned with hiding the message, but rather authenticating it. For this purpose, public and secret keys are used in opposite roles.

If I have a document I want to sign, I encrypt it with my secret key and send it to the other party. The other party uses my public key to decrypt the message and reads it. I can send a plaintext copy of the message along so that they can check that they match. I am the only one who could have encrypted something that my public key would decrypt, because I am the only one with the secret key. The other party can then be confident that it was only me who could have signed the document.

In practice, signing the whole document in this fashion would yield a signature block larger than the document. A neater solution is to create a "message digest" first. Before signing a document, the crypto software would compute an unique identification number for that document. The mathematical algorithm for doing this is well known, so that anyone else can take the same document perform the same math and end up at the same unique number. We call this process "hashing." Once I have a message digest (much smaller than the original document) I can sign (encrypt) it using my secret key. I would then encrypt the whole package (original document and signed message digest) with the public key of the other party and send it to them.

The other party could in turn decrypt the package using their secret key and would see the document and a signed message digest at the bottom. To verify that I sent it they could decrypt the signed message digest to reveal the plain message digest. The final step is to take the document and compute the message digest for themselves. If their message digest matches my message digest (which they have decrypted) then they can be confident that I signed the document. It would also be difficult for me to refute that I signed the document because only I have the secret key that was used to sign it.

We could still debate *when* I signed it, and this is why a trusted and accurate time stamp is often added.

Pretty Good Privacy (PGP)

A commercial product called Pretty Good Privacy (PGP) is an example of the previously described method of secure communications that is the de facto standard for secure e-mail. You can download this application for free off the Internet. The security of any encryption system is highly dependent upon the size of the key. The bigger the better in terms of security, but also, the bigger the key is, the more time it takes to process your communications traffic.

Asymmetric encryption has one drawback: it is slower than symmetric key cryptography. So some smart person had the idea to start the communication using asymmetric key pairs and use it to pass a shared secret (symmetric key) between each party, then change to symmetric key cryptography to pass real messages. Sounds great — just a few details still to work out.

Not everyone has created a public and secret key pair from scratch. A practical application of public key cryptography more transparent to the user is coming to a Web browser near you. The emerging technologies for e-commerce are secure sockets layer (SSL), Web certificates, and public key infrastructures (PKI).

Secure Sockets Layer (SSL)

Every modern Web browser is capable of a cryptographic exchange of information using secure sockets layer (SSL). SSL is a protocol that makes it possible for total strangers to communicate securely without knowing anything about crypto-security.

Look in the lower corner of your Web browser next time you are on the Internet. You will see an icon of an open lock (or one that is crossed out, or none at all). This indicates an insecure session, where all the data flowing between your computer and the Web site (server) you are surfing are passed in the clear text. If you go to a Web site and start an online purchase, this lock should close. This means that the communication is now encrypted. Clicking on the lock with the mouse will pull up additional information on the exchange. And that is all there is to it. The process happens nearly instantaneously and simply. The client does not have to do anything extra to initiate a secure communication.

The objective for designers was to hide the gory details of public key cryptography from the user or client, placing the onus on the merchant's server to initiate the exchange. The problem is that it is difficult for the customer to discern whether everything is indeed secure.

SSL is an accepted protocol for the exchange of keys and the establishment of a secure communications session between the client's Web browser and the merchant's Web server. It in no way guarantees how well the merchant safeguards this information after the exchange, nor does it take care of your computer security. Those are its limits. What it does do very well is protect the confidentiality and integrity of this communication between the client and the server, as well as check for authenticity and in some cases ensure non-repudiation.

It is useful to understand a little of how SSL works because you will undoubtedly be using it in your daily life, many times without knowing it. Take the situation where you are browsing Web pages having to do with selling stuff. At a certain point you will hyperlink to a page with the extension "htmls" instead of "htm" or "html." The "s" stands for "secure." This suffix will trigger your (client) Web browser to request a secure session from the server.

Your browser automatically sends some administrative data to the server that indicate which version of SSL software you are using (only version 3.0 is secure at the time of writing), which cipher suite (encryption method, key length) your computer is prepared to accept, some random characters, and a session identification number. Your browser also requests that the server show some credentials proving they are who they say they are.

The server reciprocates with all the same data and submits its own credentials to your computer in an electronic form called a certificate.

Web Certificates

Before you get too far along in conversation with a remote site you will want to see some identification. The server cannot produce just any ID. They are expected to use a Web certificate to identify themselves. A Web certificate is an electronic document that contains particulars such as a person's name, domain name, e-mail address, cipher suite, and so on. Most important, it contains his or her public key. To ensure that someone cannot masquerade as the server, the server's public key is signed and time stamped by a trusted third party called a certificate authority known to you and the server. It is the same idea as having a document notarized.

The SSL Process Continues

The client Web browser receives the server's certificate and a signed message digest. The client can verify the authenticity of the server's public key by verifying that it was indeed signed by the certificate authority (whose public key is usually pre-installed on the browser). You can also check the expiration date.

The next step taken automatically by your browser during an SSL exchange would be to verify that you are the rightful owner of the server public key. It does this by computing the message digest and comparing it with the signed message digest that you had decrypted.

Now that you have authenticated the server and know that they are who they say they are, you can exchange secrets. If required, as when filing tax returns electronically for example, the server can ask you to authenticate yourself in the same way.

The secret number can then be used as the key in a symmetric cryptographic algorithm that is used to encrypt all traffic from now on.

There are still some final details to clean up. A bad guy would have difficulty reading the messages between you (the client) and the server, but theoretically still could mangle a few messages by inserting noise or random data into the communications channel. Every packet of data is numbered, in a way that is not predictable to an outsider, in order to prevent messages from getting lost, or nasty ones getting inserted. A message digest is constructed for every message and is signed using the shared secret key. This way it is very difficult for an outside threat agent to change a message without being detected.

Brute-Force Code Breaking

The SSL protocol (3.0) is generally considered to be secure. There are two remaining exposures in a system using SSL, however. One involves using a weak cipher suite. This is an algorithm or key length that can be broken through brute-force cryptanalysis or fancy code-breaking schemes. Many older Web browsers or foreign export versions have weak cipher suites defaulted. But any encryption is far better than no encryption at all.

In 1997, a specific assessment of the security of typical encryption keys shows that one may be factored for less than one million dollars in cost in eight months of effort. It is currently believed that an RSA 512-bit key length no longer provides sufficient security for anything other than short-term needs.

RSA laboratories currently recommend key sizes of:

» 768 bits for personal use
» 1024 bits for corporate use
» 2048 bits for valuable keys, such as the root key pair of a certificate authority

Beyond SSL

The other place where the security of a system that uses SSL is challenged is in the way the information is handled at the client and at the server outside of the SSL channel. To illustrate this exposure, take the case of an online financial transaction where you purchased something from a company's Web site using your Web browser and SSL. Let us assume that the communication of your credit card information was secure. At some point the Web server at the company you are making your purchase from will have to decrypt your credit card information in order to use it. Here, in plaintext form, it is vulnerable. If for instance, the Web site was compromised, a threat agent may get access to this sensitive information by getting into company data banks.

Ideally, your credit card or personal information should be re-encrypted immediately on the server, and the software (or hardware) processes required to perform this function should be tamper-proof. This is most often not the case — most people's sensitive data are stored *un*encrypted.

Real-Time Credit Card Authorization

Once the company has your credit card number they need to complete the transaction. This is often performed using software designed for this purpose. Their server talks with the bank's server to verify your card number and expiry date. A notice of a valid card or conversely an unsuccessful transaction is passed back to you, the client, nearly instantaneously after you input your card information. The credit card company credits the merchant's credit card account and debits yours.

This process can be totally automated, fast and efficient, but is it totally secure? The answer is that you will likely never know. Although the communication between you and the merchant's server may be secure using SSL, there is no guarantee that the merchant communicates securely with the credit card broker or bank, nor that they store your records in a secure manner.

In January 2000, a hacker claimed to have stolen over 300,000 credit card numbers from CD Universe, an online music retailer. The thief posted 25,000 card numbers on the Internet Web site after the company refused to pay a $100,000 ransom. The would-be blackmailer said that he had obtained the data by exploiting a flaw in the site's credit card processing system.

SSL is based largely upon Internet and Web technologies that have been notoriously vulnerable to network exploitation. It is therefore imperative that an online vendor have good network security before implementing SSL-based e-commerce solutions. The entire process must be secure; there can be no gaps or exposures — "the chain is only as strong as its weakest link."

The other area in a "secure" transaction where users are called upon to take a leap of faith is in the veracity of the Web certificate. We trust that the certificate authority has checked out the company in detail and that its certificate has not been fraudulently obtained or revoked without our knowledge. Often a certificate is signed by some organization you have never heard of. Their certificate was then in turn signed by someone else, and so on and so on, until this chain finally reaches an organization you recognize. What assurance do you have in this chain of trust?

Public Key Infrastructures (PKIs)

A public key infrastructure (PKI) issues, updates, revokes, and manages Web certificates in a way that conforms to accepted industry standards. The infrastructure is formed of certificate authorities (CAs) that cross-certify each other to form a Web of trust. They act as trust brokers or notarizing authorities. To date, there exist PKIs for certain user groups, but as yet there is no single, trusted infrastructure that we all can use confidently. It is coming, but in the meantime we will have to accept some risk associated with Web certificates.

The whole encryption process makes the threat agent's job very difficult indeed, if they are interested in reading the material they steal or eavesdrop on. A threat agent must first gain a measure of access, then intercept a communication or acquire the information from storage on the targeted machine. These steps alone are tough enough for most attackers to perform successfully. Faced with encrypted files, the attacker has two choices: either find a way around the encryption, or go through it. By "going around" the encryption, I mean capturing the data before encryption takes place or after someone decrypts it for you. This often involves manufacturing additional access. "Going through" the encryption necessarily involves cryptanalysis or code breaking. Simple passwords can be cracked in seconds, but a threat agent could spend their lifetime trying to crack industrial or military grade crypto-systems.

Some of the most trusted encryption algorithms are ones that have been made available to public scrutiny and are available to you for free. Conversely, weaknesses in public key crypto-systems will be revealed publicly well before common threat agents like hackers would have the ability to mount a successful direct attack against a given crypto-system. There are ongoing code-breaking challenges hosted by academia and business. This way, software companies can more accurately assess the security of the products they are selling.

RSA-512 Cracked

In response to one of these challenges, in August 1999, a group of researchers completed the factorization (breaking) of the 155-digit (512-bit) RSA Challenge Number. This effort used 292 computers, including heavy-duty SGI and Sun workstations, in 11 sites around the world, and took the calendar equivalent of 3.7 months. While this would appear to be beyond the capability of most threat agents, this code-breaking achievement did show that 512-bit keys are not entirely secure.

Generally speaking, there are two types of cryptanalysis attacks. One involves the use of mind-numbing post-graduate math to dismantle the code and reconstruct the key. The other uses brute force — trying every possible key as quickly as possible to find a match.

The goal of a cryptanalysis attack is not only to reveal the targeted plaintext, but also to extract the secret keys for further decrypting of the ciphertext. Attacks of this nature can be mounted not only against encryption schemes, but also against digital signatures, hashes and random number generators. The cryptanalyst may only have a sample of plaintext with the enciphered text, or just the encrypted data stream to work with. The best scenario for the threat agent is to be able to adaptively select the plaintext to be enciphered and be able to collect the outputted encrypted data. Something like an adaptive chosen ciphertext attack or differential-linear cryptanalysis is beyond the access and skill level of the average hacker. These sorts of efforts are conducted by governments, or mathematicians with a bit of time on their hands.

Conclusion

Like cybernauts launched in exploration of virtual space, the average computer user connects to the Internet with little to no knowledge as to what awaits them.

By far, most of what occurs in cyberspace is legitimate or benign. The benefits far outweigh the liabilities, but to surf where there are sharks or drive down the information highway without seatbelts is simply unwise. There are serious threats lurking in the Internet and in most cases it offers threat agents an embarrassment of riches — too many naïve users and vulnerable systems and not enough time in the night.

Computer security is a lot like self-defense. You can spend a lifetime studying martial arts but you do not need a black belt in kung fu to get by on the street. I am talking about common street sense in the real world that needs to be imported into our on-line practices. The average person would think twice about entering a bike gang's club house alone at night to buy contraband, but apparently would not hesitate to download pirated software from a hacker's web site or distribute large joke file attachments containing viruses. Users ought to approach cyberspace with the same mind set and ethics as they do in the real world — watch where you visit, don't talk to strangers and restrict access to your computer as you would your home. The more you dabble in shady areas of computing the more likely you are to get burned. It is advisable to modify any unhealthy habits and practice safe surfing.

The vast majority of attacks on the Internet are indiscriminate in nature — random acts of violence. However, no one it seems will be left untouched. According to typical incident and network intrusion monitoring statistics every connection to the Internet is on average "touched" once every 24 hours by a threat. There is a 95 per cent chance that you will be subjected to a vulnerability scan from an automated program launched by some "script kiddie." It is unlikely that you will detect this activity — it is much the same as a thief rattling the doorknob on your house to see if it is locked. It is only with sophisticated intrusion detection systems that we are able to see what is actually occurring on networks. What you can't see can hurt you! The next most likely threat is that posed by malicious code, like viruses. Chances are that you will be infected by a friend or colleague.

The good news is that the most frequent threats are also the most easily mitigated by basic safeguards like installing the latest vendor patches, virus checkers, and personal firewalls, using hard-to-guess passwords, and restricting the default options on Web browsers.

Knowing the dangers in cyberspace is a good start to shedding the naïveté that many of us have when cruising the information highway and can get us into trouble. Virtual threats have real world consequences. Don't let yourself be either seduced or demoralized by complex technology. Although the tools and means of typical threat agents change almost daily, their motivations remain predictable. A thief acts like a thief, whether they use a crowbar or keyboard to steal your property. I asked a forensic accountant how she coped with an investigation that led into an electronic quagmire of interconnected computers and data banks. She replied matter-of-factly as if technology were not the issue: "I just follow the money, as always."

The value of information is one of the most overlooked facets of a computing environment. Many users grossly underestimate the direct and indirect costs of information modification or loss. Take a moment to consider losing everything on your computer. Now consider backing up your data at least once a week for peace of mind.

The degree to which you should manage risks depends upon your computing environment. The major factors that affect overall risk are the existing system vulnerabilities including the people, processes and technology, the nature of the threat activity, and the potential impact of compromise, loss or destruction of information (soft) or hard assets. A recreational home user may approach Internet security with a carefree attitude and accept minor consequences as they may occur. However, if you are either conducting e-commerce activities or relying on computers to do business, then you ought to consider the notions of security and take the cyber threat seriously. Here is a summary of the basic steps you should take:

Do a risk assessment.
Analyze your computer system and determine your vulnerabilities. Do a cost-benefit analysis to determine what reasonable steps you can take to mitigate the risk.

Establish safe practice policies.
Determine preventive measures to be taken to protect yourself, your family, your employees and your business from online threats.

Raise awareness of security issues.
Inform yourself, your family members and employees of potential hazards of Internet use.

Provide training in proper use of computer systems.
Understand and use e-mail and Web browser functions properly.

Back up all important files regularly.
Establish a backup schedule and stick to it. Keep backup files in a secure location.

Install protective software.
Use programs such as antivirus scanners, filters, and firewalls to limit exposure to Internet threats.

Update software to include new security patches.
Keep informed about security holes and bugs in the software you use to access the Internet.

Use encryption.
Learn how to keep important files and communications private through cryptography.

Develop strategies for handling incidents.
Have a comprehensive plan for handling incidents such as intrusions and virus infections.

access control: a security mechanism that restricts entry to a computer, network, application, or service based upon a set of rules.

active attack: an attack that makes a change in the target's computing environment or information.

application-level proxy: a firewall proxy that verifies the type of information passing the firewall.

assurance: a quality of an information system that establishes a level of confidence in the security system.

attack: a deliberate action by a threat that is directed against a vulnerability.

audit trail: a chronological record of operations and actions performed on or by your computer system that have security implications.

authentication: a quality of an information system that verifies the identity of a user, process or computer.

authorization: a mechanism that ensures that the right users, processes, or machines are permitted. Authorization necessarily includes performing authentication and crosschecking identity with a list of permissions.

back door: a hole in a system that was deliberately left in place and that can later be used to circumvent security controls.

basic input output system (BIOS): provides the interface between computer hardware and software. It provides the most basic set of instructions in the computer.

breach: a defeat of the security safeguards protecting a computer or network.

buffer overflow: more data is entered in a field than expected (address too long), the computer sometimes reacts by crashing or executing the overflowing string. Deliberately overflowing the buffer is one way threat agents gain entry into systems.

bug: an undesired glitch or problem in software.

CA. See certification authority

CANCERT (Canadian Computer Emergency Response Team): their mission is to be the trusted center for collection and dissemination of information related to networked computer threats, vulnerabilities, incidents and incident response for Canadian government, business and academic organizations.

certification authority (CA): an organization that people trust to issue certificates.

certificate policy: rules and security requirements by which the CA abides.

certificate practice statement: a statement of the operating practices a CA follows when issuing or managing certificates.

circuit-level proxy: a process whereby information is passed indirectly through a firewall by copying traffic at one port and recreating it at another. The data do not pass directly through.

compromise: computing assets have been deliberately exposed or have already been successfully attacked.

confidentiality: assuring the meaning or content of the data is protected from disclosure.

countermeasures: reactions to thwart an attack.

covert channel: a disguised conduit for transporting information in an unauthorized manner.

crack (verb): to break a code; brute-force cryptanalysis.

crash: a catastrophic failure of a computer system.

cryptography: the science of code making and rendering plaintext unintelligible or decrypting messages back to intelligible form.

data encryption standard (DES): a cryptographic algorithm published in Federal Information Processing Standard (FIPS PUB 46) and approved by the National Institute of Standards and Technology (NIST) used by the public and governments.

decryption: the process of decoding a message to its original plaintext form.

denial of service (DoS): An attack which intends to shut the computer or network down.

digital signature: using a secret key to encrypt known data. Anyone can decrypt the data and verify that only you could have signed it.

domain name system (DNS): mapping of IP address numbers with domain names.

encryption: a process that renders data unreadable, except with the right keys, or allows for digital signatures, thus providing confidentiality and authentication services.

file transfer protocol (FTP): a service used to transfer files between computers over a network.

firewall: hardware or software that operates like a traffic cop; regulating the direction and flow of traffic between domains.

hacker: a threat agent that exploits information technology with computers for its own sake.

host: a computer on a network.

hash: a cryptographic operation to compute a unique number to represent a message.

integrity: assuring that information will not be changed in an unauthorized manner.

intrusion: the attacker gaining entry into your computing domain.

IP spoofing: deceiving the system with data packet containing a false return IP address.

key: a secret or public number used in cryptography.

message authentication code (MAC): a one-way hash function that has been signed with a shared secret key.

non-repudiation: the ability of both parties in a transaction to prove that a specific transaction took place at a given time.

packet filtering: routers vet the type and destination of data traffic flowing in and out of a network.

passive attack: actions taken by the threat agent which do not alter the targets information or computing environment.

penetration testing: security professionals are paid to break in to a computer system in order to test the security mechanisms.

ping: Packet Internet Groper is a slang term for a short "hello are you there" message (ICMP ECHO) sent by a computer.

ping of death: the use of Ping with a packet size higher than 65,507 bites which causes many computers to crash.

PKI (Public Key Infrastructure): the business of managing cryptographic certificates and establishing a chain of trust for online transactions.

port: one of 64,000 numbers used by TCP/IP computer network communication protocols as sub-addresses on your computer.

probe: to solicit a response from computers over a network and gather intelligence.

risk assessment: a detailed analysis of the various threats, vulnerabilities, exposures, impact and likelihood for a specific computing environment, in order to identify and calculate risk and develop security safeguards.

RSA (Rivest-Shamir-Aldeman): an asymmetric public-key cryptographic algorithm.

SATAN (Security Administrator Tool for Analyzing Networks): an automated vulnerability-scanning program.

sniffer: a device that taps a data network.

spoofing: manipulative deception involving information.

SYNflood: a type of denial of service attack.

TCP/IP (Transmission Control Protocol/ Internet Protocol): network and transport-level rules that allow computers to communicate with each other.

threat agent: the bad guy.

threat event: the bad thing the threat agent does.

trap door: hidden access to your computer system.

Trojan horse: a program, usually malicious, hidden within a legitimate program.

virus: software that copies itself, spreads and does damage.

vulnerability: an intrinsic property of a computer system or network that can be exploited by threat agents.

Selected Bibliography

American National Standards Institute. *Data Encryption Algorithm,* ANSI X3.92, 1981.

———. *Digital Signatures Using Reversible Public Key Cryptography for the Financial Services Industry,* ANSI X9.31, 1998.

———. *Financial Institution Message Authentication,* ANSI X9.9, 1986 (Reaffirmed 1994).

———. *Financial Institution Retail Message Authentication,* ANSI X9.19, 1986 (Revised 1996).

———. *Public Key Cryptography Using Irreversible Algorithms Part 1: The Digital Signature Algorithm (DSA),* ANSI X9.30-1, 1993 (Revised 1997).

———. *Public Key Cryptography Using Irreversible Algorithms Part 2: The Secure Hash Algorithm (SHA-1),* ANSI X9.30-2, 1993 (Revised 1997).

———. *Financial Institution Key Management (Wholesale),* ANSI X9.17, 1985.

American Society for Industrial Security (ASIS) & Pricewaterhouse Coopers. *Trends in Proprietary information Loss Survey Report.* October 1999. www.pwcglobal.com.

Atfield, P., Breakspear, A., Denton, T., Robbins, J. "Business Information Operations." Tutorial at the Canadian Information Technology Security Symposium. June 1999.

Attrition.org. "Defacement Statistics." www.attrition.org.

Bourque. Colonel J.D.R. Information Operations for Canada. www.cfcsc.dnd.ca/irc/amsc/smsc1/003.html .

Bronskill, Jim. "Canada a key snooper in huge spy network," *The Ottawa Citizen,* 24 May 1999.

Bugtraq Vulnerability Database Statistics. www.securityfocus.com /vdb/stats.html.

Campbell, Duncan. "Intercept Capabilities 2000." April 1999. www.cyber-rights.org/interception/stoa/interception_capabilities_2000.htm.

Canadian Broadcasting Corporation (cbc.ca). "Sempra to distribute gas; misdirected e-mail leaks decision." Posted 15 December 1999. cbc.ca/cgi-bin/templates/view.cgi?/news1999/12/15/nsemailmiss151299.

Canadian Computer Emergency Response Team (CANCERT). "1999 and 2000 Threat Briefings to Industry." www.cancert.ca.

Canadian Security Intelligence Service. Annual Reports and Commentaries. *Computer Security June 1999, Economic Espionage June 1999, Economic Security 24 Jan 2000, Information Operations (the cyberthreat) 1999.* www.csis-scrs.gc.ca.

Canadian Security and Intelligence Review Committee. "Annual Review of CSIS Intelligence Activities." www.sirc.gc.ca.

Charles, Deborah. "Clinton signs digital signature bill," ZDnet, 30 June 2000. zdnet.com/zdnn/stories/news/0,4586,2597132,00.html

Communications Security Establishment (CSE). *Threat and Risk Assessment Working Guide.* (ITSG-04) October 1999.

———. *Network Security: Analysis and Implementation.* (MG-01) January 1996. www.cse-cst.gc.ca/english/manuals/mg1int-e.htm.

Criminal Intelligence Service Canada. *Technological Crime Report 1999.* www.cisc.gc.ca/cisc99/techno.html .

Criminal Intelligence Service Ontario, Strategic Intelligence Section. *Introduction to Information Technology Crime.* 4 July 1998.

Department of Justice (Canada). *A Survey of Legal Issues Relating to the Security of Electronic Information.* http://canada.justice.gc.ca/Commerce/toc_en.html.

Department of National Defense (DND). *Canada's Critical Infrastructure: An Overview.* National Contingency Planning Group, DND, May 1999 www.ncpg.gc.ca/toctff1_e.html.

Department of National Defense. *White Paper on Information Warfare.* Produced by EWA-Canada Ltd for DND. 09 May 96.

Dierks, T. and Allen, C. *The TLS Protocol Version 1.0.* RFC 2246, January 1999.

Disaster Recovery Journal. www.drj.com/drj2/drj2.htm.

Dobbertin, H. *Cryptanalysis of MD5 Compress,* 2 May 1996.

Dunn, Ashley. "Of keys, decoders and personal privacy,"The New York Times on the Web, 1 October 1997, www.nytimes.com/library/cyber/surf/100197ming.html

Electronic Warfare Associates Canada. (EWA-C). *Report on the Threats to Selected Government of Canada Internet Sites.* Prepared for the Communications Security Establishment. 17 November 1999. www.ewa-canada.com.

Ellison, C. *Establishing Identify Without Certification Authorities.* 20 July 1996.

Entrust Technologies Ltd. "Digital Certificates," www.entrust.net/ learning/digitalcerts/index.htm.

———. "Secure Sockets Layer (SSL)," www.entrust.net/learning/digitalcerts/securesockets.htm.

Federal Bureau of Investigation. www.fbi.gov.

Forum for Incident Response and Security Teams. www.first.org.

Freeh, L.J. *Threats to U.S. National Security,* FBI , 28 January 1998.

Freier, A. et al. *Internet Draft — The SSL Protocol Version 3.0,* 18 November 1996.

Garigue, Robert. *On Strategy, Decisions and the Evolution of Information Systems. Technical Document.* DSIS DND Government of Canada, 1992.

Garigue, Robert. *Information Warfare — Theory and Concepts.* Ottawa: Office of the Assistant Deputy Minister — Defense Information Services, DND, Goverment of Canada Report, 1995.

Garigue, Robert. *Information Warfare: Developing a Conceptual Framework. Discussion paper.* www.carleton.ca/~rgarigue/ paper.zip.

Goldberg, I and Wagner, D. *Randomness and the Netscape Browser.* January 1996.

Gordon. B. "Information Operations News." Mail List. www.ewa-canada.com .

Government of Canada Chief Information Officer. "GoC PKI Initiative." www.cio-dpi.gc.ca/pki/Initiatives/initiatives_e.html.

Government of Canada. Speech from the Throne, September 1997.

Hughes, E. *A Cypherpunk's Manifesto,* 9 March 1993.

Hughes, J. "Brief Comparison of SSL, S/MIME and IPSEC Security," 26 February 1998.

Industry Canada. "The Canadian Electronic Commerce Strategy. Task Force on Electronic Commerce." www.e-com.ic.gc.ca/ english/ecom_eng.pdf.

International Journal of Intelligence & Counterintelligence Low Intensity Conflict & Law Enforcement. www.frankcass.com/jnls/lic.htm.

Internet Assigned Numbers Authority, Port Numbers, 5 November 1999 http://www.isi.edu/in-notes/iana/assignments/port-numbers.

Institute for the Advanced Study of Information Warfare. www.psycom.net/iwar.1.html.

Kahn, D. *The Code Breakers.* New York: MacMillan Company, 1967.

King, C. "Building a Corporate Public Key Infrastructure." http://www.infoseceng.com/corppki.htm.

KPMG. 1999 Fraud Survey Report. www.kpmg.ca/isi/v1/frsur99c.htm.

Lasica, J.D. "The net never forgets: everything you've ever posted online could come back to haunt you someday." Salon.com

Leonhard, Woody. "The new Internet security threats," *Smart Business* (www.smartbusinessmag.com), July 2000, pp. 102-16.

Ludwig. Mark A. *The Giant Book of Computer Viruses.* 2nd edition. American Eagle Publications, June 1998.

National Information Protection Center. www.nipc.org.

National Security Agency. Information Systems Security Engineering Handbook. 28 February 1994.

Netscape Communications Corporation. "Introduction to SSL." http://developer.netscape.com/docs/manuals/security/sslin/contents.htm.

Niemczuk., J. "Defense in Depth Overview." 17 August 1998 www.nsff.xservices.com.

Office of the Auditor General of Canada. "Chapter 19 — Electronic Commerce: Conducting Government Business via the Internet," December 1998.

President's Commission on Critical Infrastructure Protection (PCCIP), 01 June 1997 www.info-sec.com/pccip/web/info.html.

Public Works and Government of Canada. Information Technology Security Directorate. *Information Technology Security Risk Management Framework Standards and Procedures.* March 1999.

Royal Canadian Mounted Police (RCMP). "Security Information Publication 5: Guide to Threat and Risk Assessment for Information Technology." www.rcmp-grc.gc.ca/tsb/pubs/reports/index.htm .

RSA Laboratories. "Frequently Asked Questions About Today's Cryptography," v4.0, 1998.

Sans Institute. "How to Eliminate the Ten Most Critical Internet Security Threats," version 1.13, 2 June 2000, www.sans.org/topten.htm.

Schneier, B. *Applied Cryptography.* 2nd edition. New York: John Wiley & Sons, Inc., 1996.

Schneier, B and Wagner, D. "Analysis of the SSL v3.0 Protocol," 19 November 1996.

Schneier, B. et al. "Secure Sockets Layer Discussion List FAQ," v1.1.1, 16 Nov 1998, http://www.consensus.com/security/ssl-talk-sec04.html .

Schneider, F.B. "Trust in cyberspace." Committee on Information Systems Trustworthiness, 29 September 1998. www.jya.com/tic,htm .

Seifried, Kurt. "Cryptographic software solutions and how to use them," www.securityportal.com/research/cryptodocs/basic-book/.

Sher, Julian. "Caught on the net: Spying gets easier," Globe and Mail, 27 February 1999.

Shimomura, Tsutomu & Markoff, John. *Takedown. The Pursuit and Capture of Kevin Mitnick, America's Most Wanted Computer Outlaw — By the Man Who Did It.* New York: Warner Books, 1996. .

Starman, R., McMahon, D., VanHees, E. "Identification and Authentication Framework for SSL Applications." Government of Canada Public Key Infrastructure, 24 April 2000.

SSCSI. "The Report of the Special Senate Committee on Security and Intelligence, Committee on Security and Intelligence Government of Canada." 1 January 1999.

Toffler, Alvin, and Heidi Toffler. *War and Anti-War.* New York: Warner Books, 1995.

Treasury Board Secretariat. "Digital Signature and Confidentiality Certificate Policies for the Government of Canada Public Key Infrastructure," Version 3.02, April 1999.

Treasury Board Senior Interdepartmental Lead Committee. "Analysis of Technology Options in Support of Secure Citizen-Centred Service Delivery." 6 July 1999.

Resources

Here are some suggestions for further reading on specific topics. The links are also available at www.warwickgp.com/publishing/cool.htm.

General

These sites have helpful pages on all aspects of computer security:

About.com — Netsecurity
netsecurity.about.com/compute/netsecurity/mbody.htm

CNET
www.cnet.com

Computer Security Institute
www.gosci.com

Security Portal
www.securityportal.com

Sympatico
www1.sympatico.ca/Contents/Computers/wgsecurity.html

ZDNet
www.zdnet.com

Garfinkel, Simson, and Gene Spafford. *Practical UNIX & Internet Security.* 2nd ed., Sebastopol, CA: O'Reilly and Associates, Inc., 1996.

Internet Security Advisor. Magazine published six times a year by Advisor media (www.advisor.com/MIS). Some articles more technical than others, but useful to anyone wanting to learn more about Internet security.

Copyright

eWatch
www.ewatch.com

Cyveillance
www.cyveillance.com

- the companies above offer a service monitoring trademark misuse on the Internet.

Digimarc
www.digimarc.com
- digital watermark service

Vyoufirst
www.vyou.com
- digital copyright enforcement software

Cryptography (see also Encryption)

Kahn, David. *The Code Breakers.* New York: MacMillan Company, 1967.

Schneier, Bruce. *Applied Cryptography.* 2nd edition. New York: John Wiley & Sons, Inc., 1996. Arguably the best book on the subject of modern cryptography methods; just a word of warning — after the first few pages you will need some university-level math courses and caffeine under your belt to appreciate the material. .

RSA

http://www.rsa.com www.rsa.com
- *a security and encryption Web site that can provide a quick fix for inquisitive minds.*

E-Commerce

Strategis
http://strategis.ic.gc.ca
- *Canadian government site with information on e-commerce*

American Bar Association.
"Digital Signature Guidelines Tutorial."
www.abanet.org/scitech/ec/isc/dsg-tutorial.html

Encryption

Anonymizer
www.anonymizer.com

Freedom by Zero-Knowledge Systems
www.zks.net
- *software that hides a Web users identity and e-mail message contents.*

Pretty Good Privacy (PGP)
www.pgp.com
- *various encryption products; free download available at* http://web.mit.edu/network/pgp.html.

Fraud

Fraud watch
www.fraud.org

National Consumers League
www.nclnet.org

- these sites offer safe shopping suggestions and reports on the latest online frauds.

Free E-mail Services

Hotmail
www.hotmail.com

YahooMail
www.yahoo.com

- two popular free e-mail services (there are many others) which you can use for "disposable" e-mail addresses.

Hacker Sites

Cult of the Dead Cow
www.cultdeadcow.com

Hackers.com
www.hackers.com

Insecure
www.insecure.org

L0pht Heavy Industries
www.l0pht.com

Network Attack Response

CERT (Computer Emergency Response Team)
www.cert.org

CANCERT (Canadian Computer Emergency Response Team)
www.cancert.ca

Forum for Incident Response and Security Teams (FIRST)
www.first.org

Packet Storm
packetstorm.securify.com

AntiOnline
www.antionline.com

SecurityFocus
www.securityfocus.com

Physical Security for Computers

Targus
www.targus.com
- security devices for laptops

Privacy Issues

American Civil Liberties Union
echelonwatch.org

Electronic Frontier Canada
www.efc.ca

Electronic Frontier Foundation
www.eff.org

Electronic Privacy Information Center
www.epic.org

Privacy International
www.privacyinternational.org

TRUSTe
www.truste.org

Bacard, André. *The Computer Privacy Handbook.* Berkely, CA: Peachpit Press, 1995.

Risk Assessment and Risk Management

United States General Accounting Office, Accounting and Informatin Management Division. "Information Security Management: Learning from Leading Organizations." (Executive Guide). Report no. AIMD-98-68, May 1998. www.gao.gov.

———. "Information Security Risk Assessment: Practices of Leading Organizations." Report no. AIMD-99-139, August, 1999. www. gao.gov.

- these two reports are intended for managers of government departments but offer helpful overviews of risk assessment and management for anyone concerned about information security:

Safe Surfing for Kids

Cyber Patrol
http://www.cyberpatrol.com/dyn_hm.htm

Cybersitter
www.solidoak.com

Net Nanny
www.netnanny.com

KidSafe (Macintosh)
http://itools.mac.com/itoolsmain.html
- various utilities for filtering the sites that kids may visit

Missing
LiveWires Design
www.livewwires.com
-computer game that teaches kids safe surfing practices.

Cyberangels
www.cyberangels.org
- organization dedicated to children's online safety

Aftab, Parry. *The Parent's Guide to Protecting Your Children in Cyberspace.* New York: McGraw-Hill, 2000.

Security Software

Virus scanners
Norton AntiVirus by Symantec
www.symantec.com

McAfee VirusScan by McAfee
www.mcafee.com

Suggested products for Apple computers
http://guide.apple.com/usindex.html

Firewalls
ZoneAlarm by Zone Labs
www.zonelabs.com

TIS Internet Firewall Toolkit
www.tis.com/research/software

Security Testing
Nmap by insecure.org
www.insecure.org/nmap
- *port scanner used by both hackers and security pros.*

Secure-Me.net
www.secure-me.net
- *automated security testing*

Filters
MAILSweeper by Content Technologies
www.contenttechnologies.com
- *filter for e-mail; sorts content according to various rules; useful for blocking spam and viruses.*

CommandView Message Inspector by Elron Software
www.elronsoftware.com
- *software to filter both incoming and outgoing e-mail.*

Norton Internet Security by Symantec
www.symantec.com/sabu/nis

Shopping Online (see also "Fraud")

American Bar Association
www.safeshopping.org

Spam

SpamCop
http://spamcop.net
- *report spammers to this site, and your complaint will be for-warded to the appropriate authorities.*

Spam Recycling Center
http://www.spamrecycle.com
- *offers free spam filters and an anti-spam newsletter.*

spam.abuse.net
- *a collection of antispam links and resources.*

Web Archives

DejaNews
www.dejanews.com

Internet Archive
www.archive.org

- *two of the largest Internet archive sites. Go to their sites and type in an e-mail address to see what has been posted by users of that address. DejaNews has instructions for having posts removed and for coding postings so that they don't get archived.*

Index

accountability of information
systems, 156
Active X, 57
air traffic control, 82
alt.2600 newsgroup, 77
"always on" connection, 26, 60.
See also high-speed Internet
connection
anonymity on the Internet, 21,
31–32, 40, 58, 65
anonymizers, 58, 146
applets, 57, 63, 120, 166, 187
application proxies, 186–87
archiving of Internet content,
44, 48
attachments. See e-mail
attack tactics, 120
auctions, online, 26, 31, 39–40,
154. See also shopping online
authenticity of information,
155, 195, 202
automated teller machines
(ATMs), 192
availability of information, 155

Back Orifice, 71, 104, 113, 144
backdoors, 111

backing up files, 173–75, 183,
212
utility programs for, 174
Bhabba Atomic Research
Centre, 74
black hat hackers, 69
blackmail, 113, 206
boink, 114
browsers, Web, 165
configuration of, 56–57, 63,
165–66
security holes in, 63–64, 165
browsing. See Web surfing
brute-force code breaking,
125–26, 204
bulletin board (BBS), 31. See
also message boards

cable modems, 17, 25–26,
60–61
cache, 63, 167
cameras, Web, 99, 112–13
Canada, 82, 85, 144, 176
Cap'n Crunch, 70
Caribbean nations, 22
casinos, online, 22
CD Universe, 206

CD-ROMs, 102, 175
certificate authority (CA), 201
CERT (Computer Emergency
    Response Team), 105,
    176–77
certificates, Web, 201, 203, 206
chain letters, 32, 36, 182
Chaos Computer Club, 70, 72
chat rooms (Internet Relay
    Chat), 40–41, 42–43, 44, 51,
    75–76
    anonymity and, 21
    children and, 40, 41
    fraud and, 31, 40, 41
    personal information and, 28
    viruses and, 107
Cheops, 137
Chernobyl virus, 105–6, 109
children
    chat rooms and, 40, 41
    Internet threats to, 5, 40, 41,
        49–50, 76, 183
    online activities of, 74–75
    supervision of, 51–52, 76
China, hacktivist attacks on,
    70–71
code
    breaking, 125–26, 204
    malicious, 102 (see also
        Trojan horses; viruses)
    mobile, 56
Computer Emergency Response
    Team (CERT), 105, 176–77
computers, theft of, 99
confidentiality, 155, 194, 202
content filters, 28, 172, 183
contingency planning, 172–77
conversation, monitoring of,
    112–13
cookies, 55–56, 63, 163,
    167–68
copyright, 48–49, 151
crackers, 69, 140
credit cards, 35, 37, 153–54
    online purchases with,
        192–93

real-time authorization of,
    205–6
theft of, 35, 56, 96–97, 193,
    205
criminal use of Internet, 65, 66,
    81–82. See also fraud
cryptanalysis, 124, 125–26
cryptography, 124–25, 195–97
    asymmetric, 197, 199,
        200–1
    public key, 193, 197–98,
        199–200, 201, 206
    symmetric, 197, 200, 203
    See also encryption
Cult of the Dead Cow, 70,
    71–72, 109
cyber-squatting, 49
cyber-terrorism, 66, 75–76,
    83–84, 89
Cybercop, 190

data loss, 172
Datastream Cowboy, 70
Defense Department (U.S.), 22
degradation of signals, 119
delay of information, 119
denial of service attacks (DoS),
    26, 112, 113, 121, 122
    third-party liability and, 61
    vulnerability to, 60, 135
digital linear tape (DLT), 175
digital signatures, 198–99, 200
disaster recovery, 172
discovery tool, 136–37
disengagement, 122
diskettes. See floppy disks
domain name, 49
domain name service (DNS)
    spoofing, 46–47, 56, 116
DoS. See denial of service
    attacks
Draper, John (Cap'n Crunch), 70
drawing an attack, 122
droppers, 104
DSL (digital subscriber line), 17,
    25, 60

Dumpster diving, 79, 95–96

eBay, 26, 39, 154
ECHELON, 85
e-commerce, 154, 161, 191–92
Electronic Disturbance Theater, 72
electronic warfare, 87–89
e-mail, 21, 160, 169–72
    addresses, 45, 170
    attachments, 54, 57, 73, 109, 170
    blocking of, 172
    "bombs", 45
    chain letters, 32, 36, 182
    corporate, 51
    as court evidence, 51
    encryption of, 124–25
    fictitious, 142
    Internet attacks and, 175
    language in, 72
    mobile code and, 57
    privacy of, 54–55
    sorting, 172
    spam, 32–35, 45
employees, use of Internet by, 50–51, 90
encryption, 124–25, 126, 151, 204, 207, 212
    asymmetric, 197, 200
    See also cryptography
error messages, 178
escrow service, online, 40
espionage, 85, 123–24
    industrial, 99
ethics of Internet use, 72–74
European Community, 85
exploits. *See* hacking programs
ExplorerZip Trojan, 105
exposures, 24, 109, 156
extortion, 65

Federal Agency for Government Communications (FAPSI), 85
files, backing up. *See* backing up files

filters, content, 28, 172, 183
firewalls, 57, 62, 129, 151, 178, 183–187
    personal desktop, 151
flame wars, 45
FloodNet, 72
floppy disks (diskettes), 102, 103, 109, 175, 182
Forum for Incident Response and Security Teams (FIRST), 176
fragmentation attacks, 113–14
fraud, 27, 32–33, 34–37, 41–42
    identity, 46
    online auctions and, 39–40
    securities, 59

global positioning system (GPS), 87–88
government networks, attacks on, 70–71, 75–76, 77–78
Groupe Segfault, 76
Guzman, Onel A. de, 108–9

Hackers (film), 68
Hackers Unite, 54–55
hackers, 26, 31, 65, 66–68, 77, 113, 161
    altruism and, 63–64, 69, 70–76, 77
    black hat, 69
    definition of, 67, 68–69
    ethics of, 71–72, 73
    groups of, 131–32
    history of, 67
    MACs and, 58
    popular culture and, 67–68
    prosecution of, 179
    public perception of, 77
    security holes and, 63–64
hacking, 68–69
    programs (exploits), 50, 74–75, 76–77, 101, 102, 111–13
    state-sponsored, 87
hacktivism, 70–73, 74
harassment, 51, 113

Harkut-ul-Ansar, 75–76
hashing, 126, 140, 200
high-speed Internet connections, 17, 25–26, 60–61
holes, security, 63
home computers, 60, 187
attacks on, 16, 25–28, 60
Hong Kong Blondes, 70–72
Hotmail.com, 45, 54–55
hypertext markup language
(HTML), 56–57

I LOVE YOU.vbs (virus), 95,
107–9
identity fraud, 46
IDS. See intrusion detection systems
incident handling, 175–78
India, 74, 75–76
information
evaluation, 42–43
properties, 155–56
security, 155
information operations (IO),
86–87
information security engineers,
18, 188
hiring, 190–91
information warfare (IW), 84, 86
insertion of foreign data,
118–19
insider threats, 49–50, 51, 65
integrity, 155, 195
intelligence gathering (spying),
85, 123–24
interception, 117–18, 194
Internet
addressing protocols
(TCP/IP), 58
history, 167
regulation, 16, 22, 56
usage guidelines, 51–52,
160–61, 211
Internet Explorer, 107
Internet Protocol (IP) address,
55, 136, 184

fragmentation, 113
spoofing, 115, 121
Internet relay chat (IRC). See
chat rooms
Internet service provider (ISP),
175, 179
interoperability of software, 109
Intrusion detection systems
(IDS), 62, 121, 151–52, 178,
188–89
inverse mapping, 136
IP. See Internet protocol address
IPfrag teardrop, 114
ISDN, 60
ISP. See Internet service
provider
ISS Security Scanner, 190

Java programming language, 57,
63, 120, 166, 187

kill session, 116
kiting, 59–60
Kosovo conflict, 87–88

L0pht Heavy Industries, 70, 140
L0phtCrack, 125, 140
LAN (local area network), 61
laptop computers, 99, 161
legal advice online, 42
Legions of Doom, 70
Li, Lemon, 72
liability, third-party, 50, 61,
110–11
libel, 43, 44–45
links, 47–48
logic bombs, 104–5
logs (firewall, IDS), 111, 138,
152, 178–79, 185
lonely heart scams, 41

machine address (MAC), 57–58
Macintosh computers, 130
malicious code. See viruses
man-in-the-middle attack, 118
masking, 121

masquerading, 118
Masse, Robert, 50
Melissa (virus), 95, 106–107
Mentor, 66–67
message boards, 42–43
message digest, 199–200, 204
meta-crackers, 70, 75
Mexico, 71
microphones, 112–13
Microsoft Office, 58
Microsoft Word, 106–7
military operations, 87
Milw0rm, 74
mirror sites, 142–43, 146–47
mobile code, 56–57. *See also*
Trojan horses; viruses
modems
attacks on, 120
cable, 17, 25–26, 60–61
dial-up, 25, 111
money orders, 39
Moonlight Maze, 86
Morris, Robert, 70
motorcycle gangs, 82

NetBIOS Auditing Tool (NAT),
140
Netbus, 104, 142, 144–45, 146
Netcat, 137
Netiquette, 44–45
Netscape, 63
network
exploitation, 87
mapping, 120
sharing, 61
newsgroups, 28, 45, 59, 166.
See also message boards
newtear bonk, 114
Nmap, 133–34
non-repudiation, 156, 195, 202

onsite attack tactics, 97, 161
operating systems, 178
operational assurance, 189–90
organized crime, 70, 75, 81–82,
86

Outlook (e-mail program), 107–9

packet, 113
splitting, 121
storm, 115
passwords, 94, 98–99, 146,
151, 161–64, 207
boot-up, 164
choosing, 162–63, 164
cracking of, 125–26
default, 125
patches, security, 64
pedophiles, 40-41
PGP. *See* Pretty Good Privacy
Phonemasters, 78–81
phrackers, 68, 78–81
phreakers, 68, 69
physical attack, 99
ping of death, 114, 120
PKI (public key infrastructures).
See public key cryptography
pornography, 51
prescription drugs, 38–39
Pretty Good Privacy (PGP),
200–1
privacy, 28, 54–56, 166–67
cable modems and, 60–61
propaganda, 84, 87, 89–90
proxies
application, 186–87
Web browsing, 58
public key cryptography, 193,
197–98, 199–200, 201, 206
pyramid schemes, 35–36

reconnaissance, 61–62, 117,
134, 135
regulation of Internet, 16, 22,
56
reliability of information systems, 156
replay attack 118–19
Reverse nslookup, 134
risk, 23, 156, 157
assessment, 17, 23, 28,
154–55, 187, 211

risk *(continued)*
    management, 17, 29, 154,
        156–58, 187
Rootkit, 140
routers, 116
RSA 512-bit key, 204, 208
Russia, 81–82, 86
    intelligence gathering by,
        85–86
    Security Service (FSB), 85

sabotage (cybotage), 82–83
SAINT (Security Administrator's
    Integrated Network Tool),
    139–40
SATAN (Security Administrator
    Tool for Analyzing Networks),
    139, 190
scams, 34
scanners
    graphical network, 137
    virus, 130, 146, 182
    vulnerability, 61–63, 112, 139
scanning, stealth, 61, 62, 70,
    135–36
screen-saver passwords, 98–99,
    162
script debugging, 166
script kiddies, 74–75, 76–77,
    83, 102
secure sockets layer (SSL),
    201–5
securities fraud, 59
security
    assessment tools, 112
    holes, 63–64, 77
    patches, 63, 212
    plans, 17, 23, 177
Shadow Project, 70
shill bidding, 39
shopping online, , 37, 40,
    153–54, 168, 192
    illegal goods and, 38–39
    returns policy and, 35–36
    See also auctions, online
shoulder surfing, 98

signature block, 199
smart bomb, 88
Smith, Dave L., 106
sniffers, 140–1
Sniper, 116
social engineering, 79–80,
    93–95, 96, 97–98, 161
software
    bugs, 63–64
    manuals, 160
spam, 32–36, 45, 58
spoofing
    DNS, 46–47, 56, 116
    IP address, 115, 121
spying. *See* espionage
SSL (secure sockets layer), 201–5
stalking, 45
stocks
    online rumors and, 42, 59
    trading online of, 58–60
stolen goods, online sale of, 38
storm, packet, 115
STORMII, 85
surfing. *See* Web surfing
symmetric key cryptography,
    197, 200, 203
synchronization request, 114
SYNflood, 114–15, 143
synhose, 115, 143
system administrators, 16, 62,
    141, 161

TCP/IP (Internet addressing pro-
    tocol), 58
telecommunications, hacking
    of, 79–80
terrorism, 66, 75–76, 83–84,
    89
threat agents, 65, 66, 157
threats, 24, 26–27, 156
    asymmetrical, 89
    insider, 49, 90–91
time, 60, 88
trademarks, 47, 49
training, 16–17, 160, 212
transactions, secure 194

Trojan horses, 71, 95, 104, 108,
    121, 145–46, 182
  ExplorerZip, 105
  tunneling, 121

United States government, 22,
    85, 86

VBS.LoveLetter.A virus (I Love
    You), 107
VicodinES, 106
virtual private networks, 192
virus hoaxes, 32, 36, 182
virus scanning software, 109,
    128, 130, 146, 182–83
virus-worm-Trojan hybrids, 105,
    107
viruses, 32, 54, 57, 102, 103,
    109, 170, 177, 182, 187
  Chernobyl, 105–6, 109
  Melissa, 95, 106–7
  VBS.LoveLetter.A (I Love
    You), 107
vulnerabilities, 24, 27, 109, 118,
    156
  scanning for, 62, 133, 139,
    189–90

wallet, Internet browser, 166
war dialers, 111
War Games (film), 68
warez, 76, 135
watermarks, digital, 151

Web browsers. *See* browsers,
    Web
Web cameras, 99, 112–13
Web certificates, 201, 203, 206
Web forms, 28, 55, 167
Web site, 32, 34, 47, 48,
    191–92, 201
  content, 47–49
  design, 33, 35–37
  hacking, 149
  hijacking, 47, 116
  passwords, 163
Web surfing, 167–69
  anonymity for, 58
  tracing of, 55–56
white hat hackers, 69
White House, 79
white-collar crime, 91
whois database, 134
Windows operating system, 61,
    104, 130
Wong, Blondie, 71
worms, 105. *See also* viruses

Y2K, 17, 97–98
Yahoo, 26
Yellow Pages, 71
You Have Mail (film), 41
Yugoslavia, 86–88, 89–90

Zhirinovsky, Vladimir, 86
Zip drives, 175
zombies, 124